Asaph Mode
Heaven has a sound. You have a part.

Edwin Santos

Freedom in His kingdom (@freedomihk)
www.freedomihk.org

Copyright © 2026 Edwin Santos

All rights reserved

The characters and events portrayed in this book are fictitious. Any similarity to real persons, living or dead, is coincidental and not intended by the author.

No part of this book may be reproduced, or stored in a retrieval system, or transmitted in any form or by any means, electronic, mechanical, photocopying, recording, or otherwise, without express written permission of the publisher.

ISBN-13: 979-8-9945527-0-4

Cover design by: Kardiakko Media
Library of Congress Control Number: 1-15075088211
Printed in the United States of America

Dedicated to all the musicians, worship leaders, FOH engineers, Monitor Engineers, Recording Engineers, Teachers, Students, Mentors, and Stage Crews I have ever had the priviledge of working with.

May you never doubt that what you carry matters, that your obedience shifts atmospheres, and that heaven hears every faithful note.

Table Of Contents

Acknowledgements	VII
Intro	XI
Prologue	XVIII
Chapter 1: The Silence Before The Solo	1
Chapter 2: The Great Vibe Check	18
Chapter 3: You Are Not Background Noise	32
Chapter 4: Comparison is the Thief of Your Awesome	50
Chapter 5: Get Your Head in the Game	68
Chapter 6: Stop Faking it	84
Chapter 7: Don't be That Guy Who Forgets	100
Chapter 8: How to Roar at Heaven	118
Chapter 9: Singing While the Ship Sinks	133
Chapter 10: Just Stop Talking and Worship	147
Chapter 11: Building Something That Outlives You	163
Chapter 12: Just Hit Play	177
About the Author	196

Acknowledgements

To my wife - Thank you for believing, covering me, and standing steady through every unseen season.

To my children - Pastor Alan, Isabella, and Josiah - you are my greatest stewardship and deepest motivation. Everything I build is for the future you will lead.

Dad, thank you for taking me everywhere with my borrowed drums when I wasn't able to drive. Mom, thank you for your tireless prayers and for reminding me that Holy Spirit guides me.

And to my coach, Lidia - thank you for clarity, challenge, and courage when I needed all three.

I did not walk this path alone.

Intro

The Guy With The Cymbals

(And Why You Should Care)

Let's be honest for a second. If you opened this book, it's probably because you feel some vibrating frequency inside you—a sound, a calling, a weird little nudge that says, "Hey, there's more to life than paying bills and doom-scrolling." Or maybe you just liked the cover. Either way, I'm glad you're here.

We need to talk about a guy named Asaph.

I know, I know. "Asaph" sounds like a sneeze, or maybe a brand of cough syrup. He's one of those biblical names you skip over when you're trying to read through the Old Testament without falling asleep. But stick with me, because Asaph is actually the coolest guy you've never heard of.

History usually focuses on King David. David gets all the press. David is the quarterback, the lead singer, the guy on the poster. Asaph? He was the guy standing next to David, holding a pair of bronze cymbals.

Now, you might be thinking, "Great. I bought a book about a backup percussionist."

But here's the thing: Asaph wasn't just keeping the beat. The Bible calls him a "Seer." That means while everyone else was just hearing music, Asaph was hearing the future. He was tapping into a frequency that nobody else could hear. He was a bridge between the noise of earth and the sound of heaven.

And I have a sneaking suspicion that you are too.

Look around. The world right now is a dumpster fire of noise. Everyone is screaming. Social media is a chaotic mess of opinions, fear, and cat videos. It's exhausting. And in the middle of all that static, you are trying to find your voice. You're trying to figure out how to live a life that actually matters, a life that feels connected to God, without being weird and religious about it.

You want to make a difference? You want to shift the atmosphere in your home, your school, your job, or your city? You need to learn how to do what Asaph did.

You need to unlock your frequency. You need to unlock your "sound".

This book isn't about learning how to play the harp or memorizing Levitical laws (thank God). It's about learning how to stand in the middle of a chaotic world and release a sound of peace, power, and authority. It's about dealing with your own junk—your envy, your burnout, your doubts—so you can be a clear vessel for something bigger than yourself.

God is looking for a new generation of Asaphs. He's looking for people who aren't afraid to pick up the cymbals and crash through the silence. He's looking for people who are done with fake, polite religion and are ready for the raw, unfiltered presence of the Kingdom.

So, grab your coffee. Put your phone on silent. It's time to get tuned up.

Welcome to the Asaph Generation. This book will show you how to get into **Asaph Mode**.

Prologue

The world was loud, golden, and seemingly perfect- and Asaph was tired. From his vantage point, the wicked didn't just survive; they thrived. Their bodies were healthy, their pockets were full, and their pride was worn like a necklace. Asaph looked at his own hands, hands calloused by the service of the God he couldn't see, and felt his feet begin to slide. "Was it for nothing?" he whispered.

Let's be real: watching people who don't give a rip about God live "the dream" while you're grinding for the kingdom is a total head-trip.

We've all been there. You're trying to stay in your lane, honoring your calling, and being a decent human being, but then you look over at the "successfull crowd. They're shiny. They're unbothered. They have their money and the vacation photos that make your life look like a beige cubicle.

Even Asaph - the O.G. of worship, the man with the direct line to the Divine - almost lost his mind over this. He straight-up admitted, "My feet had almost slipped." He was one "comparison-trap" away from throwing in the towel and saying, "Forget this God stuff, I'm going where the money is."

It wasn't until he stepped over the threshold of the Sanctuary that the music changed. In the presence of the

Eternal God, the "glitter" of the world lost its shine, and Asaph found his "sound" again.

If you're tired of feeling like your calling is a chore while everyone else is having a party, welcome to the Sanctuary. It's time to stop looking at their "gold" and start finding your "sound."

It's time to flip the switch. It's time for Asaph Mode.

EDWIN SANTOS

CHAPTER 1

THE SILENCE BEFORE THE SOLO

Tuning The Messy Start

Let's start this whole conversation with my own glorious failure.

I've been everything in the church, and I mean everything but the guy who actually gave the sermon. But if you want to talk about how I started, let's go way back to the lowly kid on the drums.

It was a fateful Wednesday night at Iglesia Evangelica Latina on Sunset Blvd in the heart of Los Angeles. I didn't know what I was doing. My timing was a disaster. My fills sounded like someone threw a sack of wrenches down a staircase. And eventually, due to the sheer dissonance and distraction I was causing, I got the boot. Kicked off the drums. The shame was real, people. I was a noise casualty.

But that moment—that moment of being rejected for making the wrong kind of sound—was actually the beginning of everything.

Here's the thing you need to get straight: God doesn't call the qualified; He qualifies the called (I know that's a tired old catch phrase but it's true). And sometimes, the process of qualification is just straight-up embarrassing. That moment when I had to step away from the kit wasn't an ending; it was the world's loudest reset button.

I went from causing dissonance to becoming, in my eyes at least, one of the best drummers in LA in the mid-90s. I played in bands, I toured, I traveled the world because of those hands that once couldn't keep a simple 4/4 beat. The trajectory was wild, but it was driven by a single, burning desire: I have to get the sound right. And thinking about it now, I didn't even know enough about the drums to know anything about keeping time or getting any kind of "right" sound from it. All I knew is that I belonged behind the drums. All I knew is that I *had* to play drums.

That hunger led me everywhere. It led me to try new things, new instruments and I even learned how to operate a mixing console and record professionally. I learned how to be a recording engineer from the bus driver for a very (formerly) famous band called Petra (shout out to the legends!). I got to witness the entire evolution of recording and how music is made—from the heavy, analogue days of recording onto analog reel-to-reel tapes to the digital dawn of ADAT machines and hard drives. Most people alive today will never get that full-spectrum view. They'll never see worship music morphing from heavy guitar riffs to dance tracks to the modern, electronic-driven acoustic sound we hear now.

But here's the kicker, the one truth that cuts through all the gear changes, the fashion shifts, and the genre hops: In all of this, the frequency that reaches our ear is the same. And the God that we serve is the same.

All that tech evolution, all that musical change, it was just the delivery system. The message, the core frequency of the Kingdom, never budged.

You may feel like that lowly kid on the drums right now —making noise, causing distraction, making people want to stop you from making noise, and maybe feeling like the world (or God) is kicking you out of the picture. Guess what? You are exactly where you need to be. I was exactly where God wanted me and so was Asaph.

Before Asaph was appointed to crash the cymbals and prophesy the future, he was just a Levite named Asaph. And that's where our story begins: in the silence, before the solo.

The Mandatory Practice Room

Before King David—the guy who literally wrote the book on worship—burst onto the scene and changed the rules of music forever, Asaph was just a lowly Levite. A Gershonite, if we're getting technical (1 Chronicles 6:43).

In simple terms, he was part of the crew responsible for the Ark of the Covenant, the Tabernacle, and the whole spiritual show. This reminds me of the times I would help to set up the sound system every Sunday morning in a school auditorium when our church was growing and we didn't fit in our little building anymore. We were a crew of 4 that would set up every Sunday morning at 6 am to make sure everything was ready for Sunday school at 8 am. We would bring in the speakers, the drums, the mixing console, the guitar cabinets and all the singer's mics. And then once the rush was over we had to get in our suits, sit in the front and wait until all 3 services were over. I did this for several years without pay, without a simple thank you but little by little I was getting closer and closer to the drums and without noticing I learned a ton of skills and had a very thorough understanding of what it took to get a typical "show" going. Looking back at this time in my life I realize that I was a practicing Levite.

But here's the brutal reality of the Levites: they had a lot of rules and a ton of waiting. They had to hit certain age markers to start service, and they had to retire when they hit fifty (Numbers 4:3). Their job, for decades, was grunt work: carrying heavy things, setting up tents, and keeping everything clean. It was manual labor with a spiritual title.

There was no spotlight. There were no social media

followers. There was just the grind.

Let me ask you: What does your current waiting season look like? Are you carrying heavy things? Are you stuck in a job that feels like grunt work? Are you just waiting for the phone to ring with the big opportunity? Or maybe you're a student that asks, "Why do I have to learn this stuff that I'm never going to use in my life anyway?"

I know how much that sucks. It feels like wasted time. It feels like God is running a massive stadium tour and you're still sitting in the practice room with a broken metronome, wishing someone would just notice you.

But here's the game-changer: The quiet seasons are not cancellations; they are qualifications.

You cannot release the frequency of God's kingdom until your own instrument—your character, your intentions, your heart, your mind—is perfectly tuned. God wasn't worried about Asaph's ability to play the cymbal; He was worried about Asaph's ability to handle the anointing that came with the cymbal. This, my friend, is what you are possibly going through right now.

Think of it like this: When I was learning to make music, I had to master two things. First, the technical skills (the drums, the keyboard, the production). But second, and far more important, was the mastering of the sound. If the recording room was full of background noise—a faulty cable, a grounding hum, a distraction—no matter how great the drummer was, the final track was ruined by dissonance, noise, or even a bad mood.

Dissonance in your life is the background hum of:

• Unforgiveness you haven't dealt with (especially toward your parents).

• The insecurity or unworthiness you keep hiding behind performance.

• The bitterness that is slowly poisoning your perspective when you see how evil people prosper and succeed while you're stuck in the practice room.

Asaph had to be qualified in the silent, thankless Levitical work so that when David finally called him up, his character wouldn't crash the anointing. The anointing, the spirit, the power, the sound—it flows through the clean channel of your integrity. If the channel is plugged up with self-pity or pride, the frequency won't come through. Period.

So stop throwing a pity party because you're stuck in the back row. This is your mandatory practice room. You are not waiting for God to show up; you are waiting for *you* to be fully tuned.

The biggest mistake you can make right now is to focus on the platform instead of the preparation. Because when that spotlight finally hits you, you won't have time to fix your heart. That messy stuff will get amplified, and the dissonance will be heard by everyone. God is using this quiet season to clean out the hum. Embrace the silence. Tune your heart. Your solo is coming.

What the practice room looked like for me

But here's the part I didn't tell you earlier—the part that proves God doesn't just restore; He reroutes with precision.

After I got kicked off the drums, the pastor's son pulled me aside. Instead of joining the chorus of people disappointed with my "ministry of noise," he took me to his recording studio (shout out LA Christian MIDI). Imagine this: I'm eleven years old, still stinging from the humiliation, still hearing the echo of those off-beat hits, and this dude sits me down in front of an Octapad. A glorified plastic square with rubber pads. It wasn't glamorous, it wasn't a real drum kit, and it definitely wasn't a stage.

But it became my training ground.

He looked at me and said, "Just keep the beat."

No judgement. No frustration. No spiritual symbolism.

Just rhythm.

And here's the crazy part: I wasn't scared. Not even a little. At eleven, I didn't have that adult fear we pick up later—the fear of failing again, the fear of looking stupid, the fear of "what if I'm not good enough?" Nah. Kids don't have that garbage. Kids go. Kids jump. Kids try. Kids follow the pull in their gut without overthinking it.

Jesus literally said that the Kingdom belongs to people like that—people who can move with childlike faith, who don't sabotage themselves with endless "what ifs." When I stepped toward those drums again, I didn't do it because I was talented. I did it because something inside me said, This is yours. Don't quit. I didn't know it at the time but that still small voice was the Holy Spirit nudging me, introducing me to His voice, His feeling, His love.

And God, being God, honored that tiny, childlike spark.

Out of my embarrassment, He sent a teacher. Out of my humiliation, He carved a learning path. Out of that Wednesday night failure, He built a runway. And eventually, He gave me a gig back at the very same church that clowned on me. That's redemption with style.

And the whole "lugging equipment around" part? Bro...

that was my Levite season. I set up and tore down gear for over twenty years. Drum kits, monitors, cables, subs, lights, mixers—you name it, I carried it. That grind shaped my character more than any sermon could. All those late-night teardowns, all those early-morning load-ins, all the sore backs, all the duct-taped cases—that was my Levitical training. My grunt work. My silent preparation.

Playing drums in different churches, bands, and ministries wasn't just experience—it was authenticity school. Every sanctuary, every youth event, every living room worship night, every out-of-tune piano, every microphone that smelled like someone's bad breath—all of it tuned me. All of it humbled me. All of it chiseled me.

God didn't just build my skill.

He built my character.

He built my endurance.

He built my ear.

He built my story.

God teaches us the importance of time and timing

God knows why He was teaching me in this particular way. A lot of the times that we were supposed to set up and tear down as a team, the team didn't show up. It was just my dad and I, sometimes it was just me. When my dad had to go to work or had a previous engagement he would drop me off at 6 am sharp. Some guys would show up at 6:30, some at 7, but I was always on time. Being on time is something my father engrained in me big time and it's something that has brought me a lot of prosperity and a lot of opportunities for growth that others have lost simply because they were not on time.

Let's get this straight. Being on time is not about calendars, watches, or the passive-aggressive panic you feel when someone texts "I'm five minutes away" only to arrive 45 minutes late like a confused cat. Being on time is about RESPECT!

Respect for people, respect for moments, and most importantly respect for God! But being too early is as bad as being late in God's eyes. The most important part is being obedient to God's word and taking steps when He asks you to. That's why it's so important to discern, and know what God's voice sounds like, what frequencies sound when He is giving you a command.

There's a story that's in 1 Chronicles 13:9-11 that should make anyone who thinks that timing doesn't matter sit down and breathe for a second. A man named Uzzah reached out to steady the ark of the Lord. His heart was pure, his intentions were good, his timing was wrong, and it cost him his life. Asaph was there, he saw it happen. Let that sink in. Asaph watched someone die, not because he disrespected God, but because he disrespected God's order and timing. It taught Asaph something we don't love to hear: Loving God does not exempt you from obeying His timing.

Asaph almost loses himself

Asaph was also a victim of not following the right timing. In Psalm 73 he admits that he almost lost himself for rushing into a conclusion that could have cost him his position in the temple, as well as the temple itself. He looked at the world, like a lot of us do now. He looked at the wicked prospering and he "compared" it to his own life, the years of toil, the years of breaking his back deploying instruments, lugging around the ark, setting up the tabernacle, obedient, steadfast he says "Surely in vain I have kept my heart pure…" Psalm 73:13. He admits that he had turned into a beast in his mind.

This is something I have definitely experienced in my life. I've even asked young people, old people, and regular folk around the world (not bragging but yes I've travelled the word), if this is something they have noticed as well and it is clear that the wicked are prospering. But the second part of that same Psalm 73 is so awesome. Asaph comes to, he wakes up from his beast-like mentality and he says, "Then I went into your sanctuary Lord God." Psalm 73:17 Asaph experienced God's presence inside the temple, and God showed Asaph the reality. The wicked don't prosper. They destroy themselves. All through my adult years I wrestled with this notion that the evil people, the wicked ones "prosper" but this prosperity is only an illusion. Asaph went through exactly what all of us go through now.

That's why Asaph hits different for me. Because before he was the prophetic cymbal-crasher, he was a Levite doing faithful work in the shadows—just like I was. Learning the craft. Carrying the weight. Showing up even when the spotlight wasn't on. Being shaped, not celebrated.

God doesn't waste the grunt work. He tunes you in the hidden places so that when your moment comes, your sound carries authority.

Respecting time is a spiritual skill

Here's the truth that nobody wants to hear: If you consistently show up late, interrupt moments, rush to conclusions or release words before they're ripe and ready, you're not a bad person. You're just untrained in God's timing. Asaph learned that revelation has seasons, worship has moments, prophecy has a clock, silence is sometimes obedience and being on time is less about discipline than it is about discernment. Coming to the correct conclusions takes time and clarity with God in His presence.

The real question

The real question isn't, are you talented? The real question is can God trust you with *that* moment? Are you tuned into what God's voice actually sounds like or are you doing what the social media influencers are feeding your mind? Can God trust you with that moment? That moment when God asks you to wait, to listen and not interrupt, to strike once, not take advantage of the moment and steal a solo?

Can God trust you with the moment when…

You're alone

Nothing is posted online

No one is watching

No one is applauding you

Obedience feels boring

Can God trust you when promotion and applause is ripe

for the taking? You could step forward and receive the glory, but you choose to stay aligned to God's timing. Timing doesn't just reveal character, it forms it and God doesn't promote talent alone. God entrusts moments.

ASAPH MODE

Let's Get Vibing

So now that we know a bit about Asaph's character and how similar he was to you and I, let's delve into his gig a little deeper. Not only was he the top worship leader at the temple, he was a father; he had kids! I like this guy's vibe because he was a regular Joe like you and I are. However, Asaph and his sons weren't just musicians; they were set apart to prophesy. Even more specifically, Asaph is called a Seer (2 Chronicles 29:30).

Let's break this down into a spiritual Venn diagram:

1. The Musician: He masters the technical skill (the frequency).

2. The Prophet: He speaks the current reality and the future truth (the message).

3. The Seer: He sees the unseen blueprint of God's Kingdom (the vision).

Asaph was all three, and he channeled them all through a pair of cymbals.

Imagine that for a second. While David was singing his latest Psalm about sheep or giants, Asaph was playing the cymbals, and those crash hits weren't just keeping time—they were declaring the future. They were literally establishing the Kingdom frequency, shaking the spiritual atmosphere, and giving everyone in the room a glimpse of God's perspective.

The sound was the weapon, and the vision was the fuel. The reason you were put on this planet is not just to be a nice person who has a hobby. You were created to be a modern Asaph. Your talent, your skill, the thing that comes easy to you, is not a coincidence; it is the physical delivery system for a prophetic frequency.

Stop Apologizing for Being Loud!

So, if you're a natural organizer, your cymbal is order. When you walk into a chaotic room, the prophetic frequency you release isn't a long sermon; it's the simple, elegant structure you bring. You are the Seer who can see the finished, organized version of the messy project.

If you're a killer communicator, your cymbal is clarity. You can cut through BS (sorry to the religious folk out there), confusion, and fear with a single, perfectly worded sentence. You are the Seer who can see the truth hiding behind the fog of lies.

The problem is, most of us have been taught to shrink our cymbals. We dim our light because we don't want to make anyone else feel uncomfortable. We call our anointing "just a knack" or "luck" because we're afraid of being labeled "too much" or, worse, "too loud."

But Asaph didn't play the cymbals with a soft hand. They were crash cymbals—loud, decisive, and impossible to ignore. They created a divine earthquake.

Your sound is not background noise. It is the frequency that God requires to establish His Kingdom in your sphere of influence. Stop apologizing for your anointing, stop trying to make your prophetic weapon sound like someone else's harp, and for the love of God, stop being afraid to be loud.

The world needs your specific frequency to cut through the static. It's time to unleash the sound only you can make.

The Reset Button You Never Asked For

We talked in Chapter 1 about the shame of being the "noise casualty"—the guy who got kicked off the drums because he was making the wrong kind of sound. But let me tell you about the ultimate, involuntary frequency adjustment that changed my whole life.

I was riding high on my own perceived skill. I was a

"religious wanna be," doing all the right things—playing the drums, the bass, doing the production, mastering the technique. I was focused on the analogue aspects of ministry: the gear, the performance, the measurable success. I was chasing the Kingdom, but only on the surface level.

I needed to learn how to let God establish His Kingdom in the terrain of my heart. Turns out, the fastest way to get your heart's terrain remapped is to have your entire physical body shut down.

It took months disabled on a bed, after going through the biggest scare of my life—brain surgery.

If you want a vibe shift, try staring at a ceiling for two months, wondering if you'll ever be fully functional again. Every priority, every ambition, every bit of ego just melts away. All the noise I had used to define myself—the band tours, the world travel, the fancy sound boards, the perfect timing—was gone. It was just me, the silence, and the fear.

And that, my friends, is when the real music started.

When your body breaks, your spirit either collapses or it finds the true frequency. I realized I had been serving the idea of God, the system of church, the ritual of ministry. I was obeying the rules, but I wasn't in a relationship. I was a religious wannabe, going through the motions, because it was easier than letting the King truly take over the messy, broken landscape of my heart.

The lesson? God will use extreme circumstances to dismantle the systems you rely on so you are forced to rely on His presence. This can be very traumatic and

scary but God has the ability to provide for you and keep your mind from going crazy. I couldn't work for months but God fed my family faithfully and we were never left alone to fend for ourselves. Like David noticed in Psalm 37, ..."yet I have not seen the righteous forsaken, nor his seed begging bread." I lived this verse in real life and although it was a difficult time, God always came through.

The 400-Year-Old Dust Trap

This brings us to Asaph and the greatest vibe shift in Old Testament history.

Before King David arrived, Israel's relationship with God was... complicated. It was locked down by a system called the Tabernacle of Moses. Think of it as the ultimate analogue setup: tons of rules, specific robes, ritual cleaning, and a massive set of "Do Not Touch" signs.

The Ark of the Covenant—the physical symbol of God's

presence, the thing that housed the Ten Commandments and held the frequency—was miles away, stuck in a storage closet in a town called Kirjath Jearim. It had been there for twenty years. God's presence was literally marginalized. Leave it to us humans to turn something glorious that's meant to roam the freedom of the world, into a little more than a box to store and use, "when the time is right" if ever.

The people were still doing religious things. They were sacrificing. They were following the rules. But the fire was gone. They were "religious wannabes" operating on the historical memory of a movement, not the current reality of the King of kings. This is the current funk of religion we are living now as a church. We forgot the power and might of the creator of the universe and we've attempted to make Him fit in the space of an hour service that's run more like a show than an important spiritual event.

The empty rituals kept the Moses "gig" alive until King David stepped up to the plate. David, the guy who was never supposed to be king, the shepherd boy who just wanted to worship—said, "This is trash. We are fixing this."

David realized the system was broken. The purpose of all the rules wasn't the rules themselves; it was access to the presence. And if the Presence was sitting on a shelf, dusty and forgotten, the whole operation was an empty performance.

The Open-Air Tent Policy

The moment King David decided to bring the Ark to Jerusalem and put it in a simple tent was more radical than any genre shift I've ever seen in music history. It was the shift from religion to relationship.

Moses' Tabernacle:

- Location: Gibeon (far away).

- Vibe: Rules, distance, fear.

- Access: Only the High Priest could go into the Holy of Holies, once a year.

- Goal: Obey the Law.

David's Tent:

- Location: Jerusalem (right in the middle of the city).

- Vibe: Immediate, open, passionate.

- Access: The King and the musicians (like Asaph) were constantly near the Ark.

- Goal: Worship the King of kings aka: God.

It was an open-air policy! He broke the system wide open.

And who was the first guy David called to head up this new, revolutionary, full-time worship movement? Asaph.

"David appointed some of the Levites to minister before the ark of the Lord, to make petition, to give thanks, and to praise the Lord, the God of Israel. Asaph was the chief..." (1 Chronicles 16:4-5)

Asaph went from a grunt-work Levite in the mandatory practice room (Chapter 1) to the Chief of the Worship and Prophetic Team in the middle of the presence! That is the great vibe shift.

You can stop being the "religious wanna be." You can stop following the dusty old rules that don't bring you closer to God. Your experience on that disabled bed—my experience in the silence after the drum kick—was God saying: I'm moving the Ark. I'm moving my presence from the external system to the internal heart.

If you want the King's frequency in your life, you have to do what David did: dismantle the old system (the old you married to sin) that keeps His presence at a distance. and invite Him into the messy, temporary tent of your heart, right now. Forget the robes and the rituals. Just show up and play.

Rules vs. Relationship

I grew up in a legalistic church where everything revolved around rules—not God, not presence, not worship—just rules. And not the kind of rules that protect people or point them toward holiness. I'm talking about man-made rules that suffocate the soul and make you afraid to even breathe wrong.

In that environment, the question was never "Did you encounter God today?"

It was "Did you iron your shirt?"

"Did you follow the checklist?"

"Did you look holy enough to impress the elders?"

If you dared wear the wrong thing on a Sunday—especially as a kid—you weren't gently corrected. No. You were ridiculed. Humiliated. Pulled aside into the dreaded "little room."

That room was like a spiritual courtroom… except the Judge wasn't God.

It was a panel of elders armed with disappointment, shame, and traditions older than the book of Leviticus.

They sat you down, stared at you like you had sinned against the entire universe, and proceeded to rebuke you. Not teach you. Not help you. Rebuke you.

After the rebuke came round two—the church council.

Let me tell you… if the elders were the "cops" of the church, the council was the Supreme Court. And trust me, nobody was getting acquitted.

I remember walking in one evening because I had dared—dared—to show up to a service without a tie.

A tie.

They looked at me like I had spit on the altar. The verdict came down with all the dramatics of a medieval trial:

"You are sentenced to one month of discipline. You will not play drums for any services."

A whole month.

For a missing tie.

Not for rebellion.

Not for immorality.

For a strip of fabric.

That's when something inside me snapped—not in anger, but in realization.

Legalism creates noise. Grace creates frequency.

Legalism punishes the outward appearance but never heals the inward heart.

Legalism makes you perform. Grace makes you worship.

Legalism measures your clothing. Grace measures your character.

That church had sound—but it wasn't a healthy frequency.

It was static.

Control.

Fear.

Shame.

The frequency of man, not the frequency of Heaven.

And that's where Asaph's story hit me later in life.

Because Asaph lived in a time when the priests had rituals, but *he* carried relationship.

They had regulations, but *he* walked in revelation.

Asaph wasn't chosen because he looked the part.

He wasn't chosen because he followed every rule perfectly.

He was chosen because his heart was tuned toward God. He carried the frequency of Heaven, not the frequency of religion.

And that's the tension we all face:

Will I worship God from a place of fear, or from a place of frequency; the frequency that relationship with God produces?

Maybe you grew up in a legalistic church like that too. Where the "little room" wasn't physical but emotional. Where the council wasn't a group of elders—it was your family, your friends, or your culture. Where every mistake was magnified and every gift God put in you was minimized.

But here's the truth:

Legalism tries to silence worshipers. But God raises up

Asaphs precisely from the places where worship was shut down.

You might have been rejected.

You might have been disciplined for man-made traditions.

You might have been judged for things God didn't care about.

But none of that disqualified you.

If anything, it sensitized you.

It tuned you.

It sharpened your ear to the difference between the frequency of shame and the frequency of glory.

God will often allow you to hear the wrong frequency first… so that when you finally hear His, nothing else will satisfy.

This chapter really dives into the "why" behind the shift. Now that Asaph has the job, Chapter 3 is where we zoom in on his specific role: You Are Not Background Noise. We'll focus on the significance of him playing the cymbals and being a Seer.

EDWIN SANTOS

The Power Of The High-End

Let's be honest: when you picture a worship team, the bassist is the engine, the singer is the star, and the guitar player is the cool kid. Where does the lonely cymbal player land? Maybe slightly above the tambourine guy.

We all have a cymbal player spot in our lives. It's that gift, that skill, that role that you know you're good at, but it feels... secondary. It feels like background noise. You think, "Sure, I can do this thing well, but it's not the main thing. I'm not the CEO. I'm not the prophet. I'm just the guy who closes the sale, or designs the website, or takes care of the kids, or plays the cymbals."

Stop it right there. *You are not background noise.*

The Alchemy of the Shimmer

Let's talk about cymbals for a second. And no, I don't mean those dusty metal discs sitting in your garage. I'm talking about the high-frequency, soul-piercing, "get-up-and-notice-me" shimmer that cuts through a literal wall of sound.

If you think your life is a bit high-pressure right now, try being a piece of bronze.

The Modern Cymbal Struggle (It's Still a Nightmare)

Even today, with all our fancy lasers and industrial ovens, making a professional-grade cymbal is a total beast. We aren't just stamping out cookies here. To get that "clear and bright" sound, you have to blend copper and tin in a delicate dance called B20 bronze.

- The Process: You heat it until it's glowing like a pissed-off sun, roll it, quench it in water (which can make the whole thing shatter if you breathe on it wrong), and then hammer the living daylights out of it for quite a while.

- The Time: In a high-end foundry today, a single master-crafted cymbal can take anywhere from weeks to months to fully "settle" and be finished.

If we—with our electricity and temperature-controlled factories—still struggle to get the perfect tone, imagine what was happening three thousand years ago when a cymbal was being manufactured.

David's Era: Literal Magic

In King David's time, having a cymbal that sounded "clear and bright" in an outdoor temple wasn't just good engineering; it was a freaking miracle. We are talking about the Iron Age, people! They didn't have digital thermometers. They had to judge the temperature of molten metal by the color of the flame. Back then, creating a set of musical cymbals could take a craftsman months to a year of grueling, manual labor.

The "Magic"

They were essentially alchemists. They were taking raw earth, fire, and sweat, and turning it into something that mimicked the sound of the heavens. When those cymbals crashed in an open-air courtyard, it was designed to slice through the low-frequency drone of chanting and bleating livestock. It was a "Hey! God is here! Pay attention!" moment.

It was rare. It was expensive. It was intentional.

You Are the Cymbal

Here's the "Aha!" moment you need to suck down like a green smoothie (low-key healthy): The brightness or high frequency sound of the cymbal is directly proportional to how much it was hammered. Think about that. The harder the beating the brighter the sound.

You aren't "background noise." You aren't the dull hum of the crowd or the static in the radio. You were forged to be the high-frequency shimmer that cuts through the BS of the world.

If the "hammering" of your life—the challenges, the heat, the pressure—feels like it's too much, just remember: it's taking you from a dull hunk of metal to something that can ring out across a temple to announce God's presence. You are being tuned. You are being refined. And once you're beaten into your frequency, nobody—and I mean nobody—is going to be able to ignore you.

In the new, radical, full-time worship system David set up (the one we talked about in Chapter 2), Asaph's primary job was the cymbal.

Wait, the Chief Musician, the Head of the entire team, the guy who gets his name in the Bible, gets assigned the cymbals? Yup. And you need to understand why.

In music production, the cymbals and high-hats are called the "high-end" or the "sizzle". They define the entire time signature and the groove in most genres of modern music. They are the click track for the human ear. If the bass drum and snare are the heartbeat, the cymbals are the crispness and the clarity. You hear them above everything else, sometimes subliminally, when they are mixed so well into the rest of the music that you don't notice them. They are the non-negotiable rhythm anchor. If the cymbals are off, the entire track sounds sloppy and dissonant.

Asaph wasn't just a percussionist; he was the "clarity officer". He was appointed to ensure the frequency being released in the presence of God was sharp, defined, and absolutely unmistakable.

Your cymbal is your specific, unique gift that cuts through the static. It could be your laugh, your ability to organize, your knack for encouragement, or your laser-like focus on data. Whatever it is, it might feel small, but when you are fully tuned, it becomes the sound that sets the groove for everyone around you. You see, it's possible that one day, the same situation that you're going through with your parents, at church, with friends or at school will become the very thing that will open the world to you, and I do literally mean the world.

The Forge of the Engineer

I used to think that the 'background noise' of life was something to be avoided, but my time behind a drum kit taught me otherwise. Playing in bands, recording on people's albums and teaching drums was getting old for me. I wasn't getting any satisfaction from touring and playing. I was using drumming to take advantage of people's generosity with booze and smoke whenever I was on a gig. It was extreme. I was picking up vices that were to my detriment. I was becoming a hunk of unrefined metal.

Beaten and Lathed

Think about a cymbal. To become the shimmering, complex instrument we hear in our favorite songs, it first has to endure a process of absolute destruction. The hunk of B20 metal is heated until it's glowing red, beaten down by heavy hammers, and then lathed—its surface literally stripped away and broken down. Its "vices" and imperfections have to be stripped off. It is through that 'torture' of the metal that its true tone is found. The same is with you and I. We go through stuff in life that will beat the living daylight out of us. But all that gunk that makes us a tarnished instrument has to get stripped away. That's God's way of turning you into the perfectly tuned instrument He has made for the world to enjoy. You get lathed to perfection.

My career followed that same brutal transformation. When I moved on from drumming and stepped into the world of audio-video installation and production, I was the raw metal. Learning to solder, burning my hands, and wrestling with complex network connections felt like the hammer and the lathe. It was painful, tedious, and at times, pure agony.

But just like the cymbal, I had to be broken down to be refined. The skills I learned from Petra's bus driver weren't just technical instructions; they were the strikes of the hammer. Those burnt fingertips and the 'torture' of the craft turned me from a man who didn't know his next move into a seasoned engineer. Because I was willing to endure the heat of the forge, my world opened up. The pain of the process didn't just give me a job—it gave me a passport, allowing my work to resonate in nearly every country on Earth. My work hasn't made it on the news or reached any fame or magnificence, but it does influence millions or people all over the world, even if it is behind the scenes.

The Divine Pivot: When Your Plan B is God's Plan A

Listen, I get it. You've got the vision board. You've got the "Ten-Year Plan." You've spent years—maybe six or seven of them—grinding away in a university library, fueled by caffeine and the promise of a corner office with a sleek ergonomic chair and a view that says, "I've arrived." You think you know exactly what the "successful" version of you looks like.

For me, that version was sitting behind a drum kit, touring the world, and living the rock-and-roll dream. That was the goal. That was the only goal. But here's the thing about the Universe: God doesn't care about your comfort zone; He cares about your expansion.

Sometimes, the thing you think is your "Plan B" is actually

the divine vehicle God is using to drive you toward an adventure you aren't even brave enough to imagine yet.

The Hammer, The Lathe, and the Heart

I had to learn the hard way that I was meant to be more than just a drummer. I had to be broken down, much like a cymbal. We've explored how crazy it is to produce or make a high-end cymbal. It's violent. That beautiful, shimmering disc of bronze is beaten, heated to a glow, hammered into submission, and then lathed—literally having its outer skin shaved off until it finds its voice. It has to be "tortured" to become an instrument.

My "lathing" happened in the world of audio-video installation. I traded my drumsticks for soldering irons and wire strippers. My hands, which I used to think were only meant for rhythm, were suddenly covered in burns and scars. It was agonizing. It was tedious. It felt like I was settling for a "trade" while everyone else was chasing the "dream."

But then, the pivot happened.

Putting First Things First

The world changed when I met my wife. Suddenly, the

"me-centric" dream of being a rock star wasn't enough. Family became the heartbeat of my life, and I realized that to honor that, I had to be willing to make a change. I had to put first things first.

And guess what? It is okay to change your mind on your career. It is okay to walk away from the path everyone expects you to take, be it the doctor, the musician, the (you fill in the blank). I've had to start over several times and I'm still standing (yeah, yeah, yeah). If you're reading this and you're feeling the itch to move on to the "next thing," don't ignore it. But—and this is a big "but"—don't you dare settle for the easiest path just because you're tired.

Get Your Hands Dirty

If you've been in a classroom for a decade and you're waiting for that comfy high-rise office, I want to challenge you: Take a chance on yourself by learning how to use your hands. There is a visceral, spiritual power in mastering a trade. Those skills I learned from Petra's bus driver—the ones that felt like "Plan B" at the time—became my passport. That "manual labor" turned me into a seasoned engineer and took me to nearly every country on this planet.

God took my willingness to get my hands dirty and turned it into an extraordinary global adventure. He took the "mundane" work of soldering connections and used it to connect me to the world.

The Adventure of a Lifetime

Don't be afraid to be the cymbal. Don't be afraid of the hammer or the heat. If you feel God calling you to pivot, lean into it. Whether you're a career student or a frustrated artist, don't just wait for the corner office. Build something. Fix something. Master a skill that requires callouses.

When you stop trying to control the "how" and start saying "yes" to the work in front of you, you give God the room to turn your Plan B into a life that sounds better than any song you ever tried to write on your own.

The thing is that we don't know what the future brings, but we know what it looks like for older people around us, our parents, uncles and aunts; they are our examples and our "seer" material. We can learn a lot from the older people around us. It's not always failure and regret with these people. Some of them have a great life. They are our modern day seers. We can see what the future might be like by taking their example and making it ours, or we can change the future a little by tweaking their life-examples for the better by making better decisions that they weren't able to make.

The ministry of the seer

I often wonder what life would've been like if I could see the future. Asaph was not only a musician and temple manager, he was also a seer. A seer wasn't someone who could just see the future, but a person who could pivot towards the right path to take and lead a bunch of people to take the right path towards God's will. I believe all of us have an innate ability to "see" what God has for us. God's future for us is positivity, goodness, abundance, radiance, and everything that lifts up life. God made us to thrive and to enjoy life. It has taken me over 30 years to figure that out. Like it says in Jeremiah 29:11,

"For I know the thoughts I think towards you, saith the Lord, thoughts of peace and not of evil, to give you an expected end."

What end are you expecting? God has literally given you a blank check to make your life the most awesome adventure with Him at the helm. The world has convinced us otherwise. Asaph almost fell into the wrong mindset when he saw how the world prospered as we saw in the last chapter. But the fact is that God knows that His plans for you are way better than anything you can plan for yourself.

The Seer with the Stick

Now, here is the plot twist, the thing that elevated Asaph from "really good musician" to "spiritual powerhouse":

"Moreover, David and the commanders of the army set apart for the service some of the sons of Asaph, and of Heman, and of Jeduthun, who were to prophesy with lyres, harps, and cymbals." (1 Chronicles 25:1)

Asaph and his sons weren't just musicians; they were set apart to prophesy. Even more specifically, Asaph is called a Seer (2 Chronicles 29:30).

Let's break this down into a spiritual Venn diagram:

1. The Musician: He masters the technical skill (the frequency).

2. The Prophet: He speaks the current reality and the future truth (the message).

3. The Seer: He sees the unseen blueprint of God's Kingdom (the vision).

Asaph was all three, and he channeled them all through a pair of cymbals.

Imagine that for a second. While David was singing his latest Psalm about sheep or giants, Asaph was playing the cymbals, and those crash hits weren't just keeping time—they were declaring the future. They were literally establishing the Kingdom frequency, shaking the spiritual atmosphere, and giving everyone in the room a glimpse of God's perspective.

The sound was the weapon, and the vision was the fuel.

The reason you were put on this planet is not just to be a nice person who has a hobby. You were created to be a modern Asaph. Your talent, your skill, the thing that comes easy to you, is not a coincidence; it is the physical delivery system for a prophetic frequency.

Stop Apologizing for Being "Loud"

So, if you're a natural organizer, your cymbal is order. When you walk into a chaotic room, the prophetic frequency you release isn't a long sermon; it's the simple, elegant structure you bring. You are the Seer who can see the finished, organized version of the messy project.

If you're a killer communicator, your cymbal is clarity. You can cut through BS (sorry to the religious folk), confusion, and fear with a single, perfectly worded sentence. You are the Seer who can see the truth hiding behind the fog of lies.

The problem is, most of us have been taught to shrink our

cymbals. We dim our light because we don't want to make anyone else feel uncomfortable. We call our anointing "just a knack" or "luck" because we're afraid of being labeled "too much" or, worse, "too loud."

But Asaph didn't play the cymbals with a soft hand. They were crash cymbals—loud, decisive, and impossible to ignore. They created a divine crash.

Your sound is not background noise. It is the frequency that God requires to establish His Kingdom in your sphere of influence. Stop apologizing for your anointing, stop trying to make your prophetic weapon sound like someone else's harp, and for the love of God, stop being afraid to be loud.

The world needs your specific frequency to cut through the static. It's time to unleash the sound only you can make. Stop Muffling Your Sound. The world is going to try to "choke" your cymbal. It's going to try to put a hand on the rim of your life to dampen the vibrations, quiet the ring, and make you settle for being polite, silent background noise. The world wants you to stay in the box of your degrees, your past failures, or your "Plan B" identity.

But you weren't created to be a muted instrument.

Look at Asaph. In the Bible, this guy wasn't just some

dude "clashing cymbals" in the back of the room to fill the space. He was a chief musician, a seer, and a leader. He didn't see himself as "just the percussionist." He saw himself through the lens of God's vision—as a vital, loud, and necessary part of the atmosphere. He knew that his noise was holy.

See Yourself Through the Creator's Eyes

We spend so much time looking in the mirror and seeing the burns on our hands, the years "wasted" in the wrong career, or the fear of making a change. We see a "technician" or a "former drummer."

God sees a masterpiece in the forge!

He sees the seasoned engineer who needed those burnt hands to gain the grit to travel the world. He sees the husband and father who prioritized his family and, in doing so, unlocked a level of blessing that a corner office could never provide. He sees a shimmering, lathed, and hammered soul that is finally ready to make some serious noise.

It is time to stop apologizing for your pivot. It is time to stop letting the world muffle your resonance. You have been beaten into shape, you have been refined by the heat, and you have been given a voice that can reach across continents.

God's will for you is to shine. It is to flourish. It is to ring out so clearly that the world has no choice but to stop and listen. Learn to see yourself the way He sees you: not as a "backup plan,' but as a lead performer in the extraordinary adventure He's written for you, your very life.

Now, go out there and make some beautiful, divine noise. After you read chapter 4 of course.

EDWIN SANTOS

When The Signal Gets Jammed

We're in the flow now, right? You've gotten the vibe shift (Chapter 2), you know your specific sound is powerful (Chapter 3), and you're ready to rock the Kingdom.

But then, you look up.

You know that feeling—you're crushing it on your passion project, you've finally mastered that tricky beat, or you launched that new business, and you feel good about yourself. Then you casually open up social media or look across the room at the other guy, and suddenly, you feel like a piece of low-budget, half-finished garbage.

That feeling is comparison, and it's the worst form of frequency jamming in the Kingdom. It floods your pure, unique channel with static, doubt, and soul-crushing envy.

We like to think of Asaph—the Chief Musician, the Seer, the Head of the whole prophetic movement—as some kind of spiritual superhero who never had a bad day. Wrong. Asaph was so human, so real, that he almost quit the entire mission because of envy. Envy of all things!

This is the entire premise of Psalm 73, and it's one of the most honest chapters in the Bible. It starts with a declaration, but quickly crashes into brutal self-doubt:

"Truly God is good to Israel, to those whose hearts are pure. But as for me, my feet had almost slipped; I had nearly lost my foothold. For I envied the arrogant when I saw the prosperity of the wicked." (Psalm 73:1-3, NIV, emphasis mine)

Stop and read that again. The Chief Musician, the guy who had a front-row seat to the presence of God 24/7, says his feet almost slipped. He almost lost his foothold on his calling and reality. If the guy who is in God's presence all the time can be a victim of this mental road block, then it's no wonder we suffer the same type of attack from all sides.

Envy is a Frequency Error, stage feedback even

When you're a musician, whether you're on the drums or the bass, everything is about time and footing. If you lose your foothold—if you lose your rhythm or the ability to hear the other musicians —you wreck the whole song. Your rhythm is your foundation.

Asaph was losing his rhythm not because the Ark of the Covenant was dusty (Chapter 2), and not because his cymbals were flat (Chapter 3). He was losing it because he was looking at the wrong stage. He wasn't watching King David and he wasn't focusing on the spirit of God. He was looking at the wicked. And from his perspective, the wicked were having a ball. He saw their prosperity, their ease, their fatness (literally, the original Greek word can mean arrogance or plumpness). He looked at the jerks who ignored God, made unethical money, and lived lavish, "stress-free" lives, and he had a spiritual meltdown. His exact thoughts? They were living the good life while he, Asaph, was working his tail off for God, getting "punished all day long" and feeling like his hard work and "pure heart" were totally pointless.

Comparison: The Original Frequency Hacker

To understand how comparison steals our "awesome," we have to look back at the first time a human was convinced that "perfect" wasn't enough. We often think of Eve's mistake as simple disobedience, but at its core, it was a failure of comparison.

Eve: The Perfection Trap

Consider the sheer capacity of Eve. In the Garden, she was the epitome of humankind, operating at a cognitive and spiritual 100% capacity that we can barely fathom with our modern "10% brains." She enjoyed an unfettered, direct connection to the Creator. She lived in a literal utopia where every need was met and every "awesome" attribute she possessed was mirrored back to her by God Himself.

Then came the Serpent—the ultimate frequency hacker.

The Serpent didn't offer Eve something she lacked; he offered her a fictional state, a sales pitch. He manipulated her frequency by projecting a "better" version of reality: "You will be like God." He convinced the smartest woman to ever live that her current, blissful state was somehow a prison of "not enough." Even with the world at her feet, the Serpent's sweet talk triggered a comparison between her reality and a lie. In that moment, comparison became the thief of her paradise.

The Neural Hijack: Why Your Brain Loves a Lie

Here is the thing about your brain: it is an incredible, adaptive machine. Through neuroplasticity, our neurons are constantly firing and wiring together based on what we *focus* on. When you spend your days scrolling through someone else's highlight reel or obsessing over "the wicked guy's wallet," you aren't just being "a little jealous." You are physically training your brain to prioritize a frequency that isn't yours.

When we compare, we trigger the amygdala—the brain's fear center. It perceives a "status threat," sending a screeching feedback loop through your nervous system. You are literally building a neural highway toward anxiety. Eve, with her 100% capacity brain, had the most sophisticated hardware ever created, yet even she allowed the Serpent to install a "virus." He hacked her frequency by convincing her that her current neural connection to God was "missing a piece."

The Intervention of the Sanctuary

Centuries later, the Psalmist Asaph fell into the same trap, but his story offers the "remedy" to Eve's tragedy. In Psalm 73, Asaph looks at the "prosperous wicked" and begins to spiral. He compares his struggle to their ease, his discipline to their indulgence. Like Eve, he began to believe in a version of reality that wasn't actually there. He was looking at the surface and ignoring the substance. You see, the wicked were showing their "best life" when in reality, in their souls, they were already lost and despised.

So what happened that brought Asaph back to reality? The Mental Intervention with the truth...

After waking up from the spell of comparison, Asaph

writes, "Surely you place them on slippery ground; you cast them down to ruin. How suddenly are they destroyed, completely swept away by terrors!" Psalms 73:18-19. The truth of their circumstance and future is bitterness dressed in fleeting prosperity.

The Hospital Bed: My new sanctuary

I know a thing or two about brains. Specifically, I know what it's like when the world's "frequency" gets cut off because of your brain.

For a long time, I was caught in the static. I was worried about how I looked to you, to them, to everyone. I was trying to play a song on an instrument that wasn't mine. But then came the life altering brain tumor and the dreaded brain surgery that saved my life. When you're lying on a hospital bed recovering from brain surgery, the "famous guy's platform" doesn't mean squat. The "easy guy's life" can't help you breathe.

In that silence, when I couldn't reach anyone and no one could reach me, I realized something: The only firm foundational relationship that exists is the one with the Creator. God was the only one who could enter that space. No one else had the clearance. No one else had the frequency. That's when the static finally died down, and I heard the pure tone of my own "awesome" for the first time. I realized that my value wasn't a sliding scale based on who was standing next to me. When I finally spoke openly to God and stopped hiding behind the facade of some wanna-be cool guy, I met the force, the source of life that completely altered my perceived reality. I woke up speaking with Him, thanking Him for giving me another chance at life. I made a habit of speaking with the Holy Spirit every morning. This made an incredible difference in my life and it's a practice that I still perform to this day. This is my temple and I visit it every day. No need for a building, no need for a tabernacle, just God's Spirit and me every morning.

Asaph's mind altering experience

"When I thought how to understand this, it was too painful for me—Until I went into the sanctuary of God; then I understood their end." (Psalm 73:16-17)

Asaph was on the verge of total spiritual collapse until he stepped into his "temple gig." In the sanctuary, the frequency of the world was drowned out by the frequency of the Divine. God intervened, resetting Asaph's perspective and showing him that the "awesome" life he thought others had was actually a slippery slope to destruction.

Eve shows us that no one is immune to the thief of comparison. If the smartest, most connected human could be "hacked" into believing she was missing out, how much more must we guard our hearts and especially our minds? Asaph shows us the way out: we must stop looking at the "fictional state" of others and step back into the "Sanctuary"—the place where we remember that our "awesome" is defined by God, not by a side-by-side comparison with a neighbor.

It was the spiritual equivalent of him meticulously tuning his analogue gear and working out his drum fills, only to see some other band with cheap, digital gear and zero talent selling out stadiums while he played to a crowd of ten.

The truth is, when you compare, you are accepting a false frequency. You are tuning your receiver to the enemy's broadcast, which always says: God is cheating you. You deserve better than this. This was literally the conversation the enemy had with Eve! "Did God say you can't eat any of the fruit?" God never said that! He made only *one* fruit off limits. The human downfall all started with a half truth.

The Anatomy of the Spiral

Asaph shows us the four-stage spiral of comparison that will absolutely derail your frequency and why not say it... your life:

1. The Observation: "I saw the prosperity of the

wicked." (He looked sideways.)

2. The Conclusion: "Their bodies are healthy and strong; they are free from the burdens of common mortals." (He assumed their external ease matched their internal state.)

3. The Self-Pity: "Surely in vain I have kept my heart pure and have washed my hands in innocence." (He devalued his own integrity.)

4. The Collapse: "If I had spoken out loud about this, I would have betrayed your children." (He recognized that his personal doubt, if voiced, would have destroyed the faith of others.)

Look at stage four. That's the real danger. Your internal whine doesn't just hurt you; it jams the frequency for the entire Asaph Generation around you. Your bitterness, your jealousy, your "Why not me?" attitude contaminates the air and the generation if you keep listening to it.

You cannot lead people into the presence of God if you are secretly convinced God is running a scam.

If you are going to be a Seer, you have to realize that you are not comparing apples to apples. You are comparing an Eternal, Kingdom Frequency to a Temporary, Earthbound Signal.

The solution isn't to try harder to be good. The solution isn't to look away. The solution is what Asaph did next, which we'll dive into in Chapter 5. He made a geographical, mental, and spiritual shift. He rewired his brain.

But for now, the lesson is simple: Get out of their lane. The moment you start looking at the wicked guy's wallet, the famous guy's platform, or the easy guy's life, you are choosing static or feedback squeal over the pure sound God wants to make through you. Your awesome is not their awesome. Stay focused on your own instrument and your own song.

When you start looking at the wicked guy's wallet or the influencer's curated "bliss," you are choosing static over symphony. You are opting for that ear-piercing feedback squeal you get when a microphone is too close to a speaker. It's loud, it's annoying, and it ruins the show for everyone.

The lesson is ridiculously simple: Get out of their lane.

- Your awesome is not their awesome.

- Your frequency is not their frequency.

- Your song is not their song.

Asaph almost lost his mind because he was looking at the wrong sheet music. Eve lost a garden because she thought someone else's song sounded sweeter. Don't be them.

When you focus on your own instrument—the unique, God-given "awesome" that was hardwired into you before you even had a heartbeat—you produce a sound that the world is literally starving to hear.

The Frequency the Earth Is Waiting For

The Bible doesn't say the earth is bored. It doesn't say creation is confused.
It says creation is groaning. Groaning is not passive. Groaning is the sound of pressure meeting promise.

Romans tells us that the earth itself is leaning forward—on its toes—waiting for the sons of God to be revealed. Not angels. Not celebrities. Not influencers. *You.*

Let that land for a second.

The ground beneath your feet, the air in your lungs, the oceans, the trees, the atmosphere itself—all of it is waiting for something locked inside you.

Not your talent.

Not your résumé.
Not your social media presence.

Your sound.

Your frequency.

The specific, unrepeatable, heaven-coded resonance God embedded into you before you ever took your first breath. You Were Tuned Before You Were Born. Asaph understood something most people never catch:

Sound doesn't just fill space—it establishes territory.

That's why worship shifts atmospheres. That's why cymbals mattered. That's why timing mattered. That's why not everyone was allowed to play. God doesn't release random noise into creation. He releases precision frequencies.

And you are one of them.

You are not here by accident.
You are not late.
You are not extra.

You are a carrier wave.

You are not a backup plan.

There is a note the earth has never heard before—because it only comes out when you walk in obedience, alignment, and courage.

Why the Earth Is Groaning

Creation is groaning because it remembers Eden. It remembers when humans ruled with God instead of hiding from Him. It remembers when sound and authority were aligned. It remembers when Adam named things and reality responded. And ever since the fall, the earth has been stuck under corrupted frequencies—fear, violence, lust, pride, distortion. That's why it groans. It is waiting for sons and daughters who will stop living muted lives.

Why the Enemy Attacks Your Sound

Here's the part the enemy doesn't want you to realize: He is not afraid of your sin. He is afraid of your frequency. That's why he distracts you. That's why he exhausts you. That's why he keeps you busy but unfulfilled. That's why he numbs you instead of killing you. Because a muted Asaph is safer than a talkative one.

The devil doesn't need to destroy you— he just needs to keep you out of tune.

Out of time.

Out of rhythm.
Out of alignment.

Because once you release the sound God placed inside you, creation responds.

Walls fall.
Atmospheres shift.
Chains break.
Generations realign.

This Is Your Moment. So here's the question you have to answer—not for God, but for yourself:

Can God trust you with your sound? Can He trust you to show up on time? To stay pure enough to carry it? To be disciplined enough to steward it? To be bold enough to release it—even when no one claps? Because the earth isn't waiting for perfection. It's waiting for revelation. And when the sons of God finally step into who they were designed to be, creation will stop groaning—and start singing again.

Stay in Your Frequency

The moment you catch yourself comparing, realize what's actually happening.

You're not being "motivated."

You're not being "challenged."

You're hitting the mute button on your own sound.

It's like walking into a room full of screaming toddlers and silencing *everyone*—not because the noise was evil, but because it was overwhelming. Comparison does the same thing to your spirit. It doesn't refine your melody; it shuts it down.

So pause. Take a breath. And remember the Sanctuary. The hospital bed—where life hangs in the balance and only what's eternal matters. The temple—where sound isn't for performance, but for presence. Sanctuary is where God retunes you. That's where your ears and heart recalibrate. That's where your rhythm comes back. That's where your assignment becomes clear again. Then—without apology, without delay—return to your melody.

Not theirs.
Not louder.
Not trendier.
Not safer.

Yours.

Because the earth isn't groaning for an echo.
It's waiting for your frequency.

And the moment you stop comparing and start releasing what God placed inside you, the mute button breaks—and creation finally hears what it's been waiting for.

Step back into the Sanctuary, recover your rhythm, and release your sound—because the earth is groaning for your frequency, not someone else's echo.

EDWIN SANTOS

The Pivot Point

Okay, so Chapter 4 was a real gut punch. We admitted that comparison is a frequency jammer, a soul-sucking vortex that makes you doubt everything, even God's goodness. You're looking at everyone else's highlight reel, feeling like your life is stuck in the outtakes. This is completely normal and a reaction that most people take in the current times.

Asaph felt it too. He was swirling in that toxic brew of envy and self-pity, convinced that being righteous was a sucker's game. His feet had almost slipped. His frequency was completely off-kilter.

But then, he pulled a move that changed everything. It's the pivot point for his entire testimony. It's the spiritual equivalent of hitting the "reset" button on your entire soundboard.

Here it is, the close up from Psalm 73:

"When I tried to understand all this, it was oppressive to me until I went into the sanctuary of God; then I understood their final destiny." (Psalm 73:16-17, NIV, emphasis mine)

That phrase: "until I went into the sanctuary of God."

This isn't just a trip to church, folks. This is a mental, emotional, and spiritual recalibration. Asaph didn't just change his physical location; he changed his perspective. He literally got his head back in the game.

Your Sanctuary Isn't a Building; It's a Blueprint

Let's clarify something crucial here. When Asaph talks about "the sanctuary of God," he's not talking about the grand Temple that Solomon eventually built (because that wasn't around yet). He's talking about the humble, open-air Tent of Meeting that David had set up (remember Chapter 2, "The Great Vibe Shift"?) right there in Jerusalem.

It wasn't fancy. It didn't have gold-plated everything. But it had one thing: the presence of God. The Ark of the Covenant was there, representing God's immediate, available presence. The Spirit of the Lord was available to him and whosoever needed Him.

So, when Asaph says he went into the sanctuary, he wasn't looking for a sermon or a ritual. He was looking for God's unfiltered perspective. He was saying, "My human understanding of fairness and prosperity is broken. I need a divine download."

For you, "the sanctuary" isn't necessarily a physical building either. It's a mindset. It's a dedicated space, time, or mental posture where you deliberately pull away from the world's noise and plug directly into God's frequency.

- Maybe it's your prayer closet.

- Maybe it's your car during your morning commute, with worship music blasting.

- Maybe it's a specific spot in nature where you feel closest to Him.

- For me, sometimes it's the quiet after a late-night session in the studio, when everyone's gone and it's just me and the hum of the gear, asking God, "What were you really saying through that last track?"

The point is, when Asaph stepped into that space of intentional connection, his entire perspective flipped. He stopped looking at the "now" of the wicked guy's prosperity and started seeing the "then" – their final destiny.

The God-Filter: Zoom Out, Not In

Imagine you're mixing a track. You're obsessing over one

tiny reverb tail on the vocal, driving yourself crazy. But then, you step back from the mixing board, listen to the whole song, and suddenly that tiny detail isn't so important. You get the big picture.

That's what Asaph did. He zoomed out.

When he looked at the wicked from the vantage point of God's presence, he saw something entirely different. He saw that their "prosperity" was like standing on slippery ground, a temporary high with a guaranteed catastrophic fall.

"Surely you place them on slippery ground; you cast them down to ruin. How suddenly are they destroyed, completely swept away by terrors!" (Psalm 73:18-19)

From the world's frequency, the wicked looked like winners. From God's frequency, they looked like fools dancing on a banana peel.

This is the power of the Sanctuary Shift: it allows you to see with God's eyes, not just your own. You stop getting lost in the weeds of your daily injustices and see the eternal consequences. You stop comparing your temporary struggle to someone else's temporary success and start measuring everything against the Kingdom blueprint.

Calibrate Your Compass

Your feelings are not always accurate. Your external circumstances are not always the truth. Your human logic will frequently tell you God is being unfair. That's exactly what happened to Eve when she bit the forbidden fruit. She "felt" like she was getting the short end of the stick. She "felt" like she was being taken advantage of.

That's when you need to activate your own "Sanctuary Shift." It's a deliberate act of choosing God's perspective over your own limited, self-pitying one.

It's like recalibrating your internal GPS. You've been driving off course, comparing your journey to everyone else's flashy ride. But when you hit the Sanctuary button, it re-routes you, reminds you of your true destination, and reveals the real terrain.

"When my heart was grieved and my spirit embittered, I was senseless and ignorant; I was a brute beast before you. Yet I am always with you; you hold me by my right hand." (Psalm 73:21-23)

Asaph basically admits, "I was acting like a total idiot, full of bitterness and ignorant. But even then, God, you were holding my hand."

That's grace, right there. Even when your head is messed

up from comparison, God isn't letting go. He's waiting for you to make the shift, to step into His presence, to let Him pull you out of the mud.

So, next time you feel that gnawing envy, that oppressive feeling of "Why not me?" – don't just wallow. Don't just scroll. Go into the Sanctuary. Find that space, mental or physical, where you can hear God's frequency above the static. Let Him show you the ultimate destiny, and suddenly, your path will look a whole lot clearer. Get your head in the game, because God has a bigger plan than your current frustration.

In my life, I let frustration take the best of me. I wanted to do everything at the same time so I would never finish any projects that I would start. I let time slip by ever so slightly. One minute became a day, a day became 7 months, 7 months became a year, a year became a decade and I was still in the same place stuck and frustrated. God showed me that I hadn't taken His invitation into the sanctuary seriously.

The "Until" Trap: Your Calling is Not a "Later" Thing

Let's be real: Most of us are professional procrastinators disguised as "planners." We tell ourselves we'll finally step into the sanctuary...

- Until the bank account has an extra zero.

- Until we lose those last ten pounds.

- Until our life looks "correct" (whatever that means).

Here is the truth: "Until" is a frequency hack from the enemy. It's a cloaking device designed to keep your "awesome" hidden in the shadows. While you're waiting for the "perfect" time, the enemy is throwing a party because a hidden light can't blind anyone. Your calling isn't a future event; it's a present-tense demand. You must enter the sanctuary now. Take your invitation into God's presence seriously now. Don't wait until you're ready. God is ready to receive you and train you in the sanctuary but you must enter it.

The Ethiopian Eunuch: The King of Immediate Action

In the Bible, there's this guy—the Ethiopian Eunuch—who was the ultimate example of "getting his head in the game." He's riding in his chariot, hears the Gospel from Philip, looks at a random patch of water, and basically says, "Hey, there's water. What's stopping me from being baptized right freaking now?" (Acts 8:36, heavily paraphrased).

He didn't need a six-week new believers' class. He didn't need to go home and "pray about the optics." He heard the truth, and he dove in. He understood that when the Frequency of Heaven hits your ears, you don't check your calendar. You move.

The addiction of "not yet".

I'll be the first to admit it: I regret not starting sooner. For years, I was stuck in the mud of an addiction that acted like a spiritual anchor. It whispered that I wasn't ready, that I was too broken, that I needed to "fix myself" before I could do God's work.

But here's the neuro-spiritual reality: You don't get clean to get into the game; you get into the game to get clean.

When I was on that hospital bed after brain surgery, "tomorrow" felt like a very expensive luxury I couldn't afford. I realized that "tomorrow" is the graveyard where most people bury their God-given potential. You don't have a surplus of time. You have a mandate.

Neuroplasticity: The "Start Now" Circuit

From a neuroscience perspective, every time you say "tomorrow," you are strengthening a neural pathway of hesitation. You are literally training your brain to be a "waiter." But the moment you take immediate action, you fire a new set of neurons. You signal to your nervous system that the "Sanctuary Frequency" is the priority.

God doesn't need your life to be "correct" to start using you; He needs your head to be in the game so HE can correct it.

Remember: "He who began a good work in you is faithful to complete it" (Philippians 1:6). Note that it says He will complete it—not you. Your job is just to show up at the starting line and stop making excuses. One of my favorite techniques to get out of the "I'll do it later funk" is using the 5 second rule made famous by one of my favorite authors, Melanie Robbins. "Whenever you want to get your brain's attention all you have to do is count to 5 but backwards, 5, 4 ,3, 2, 1." Your brain is not used to counting backwards so you bring it to attention by counting from 5 to 1. Once your brain is at attention you're good to go and make it start whatever it is you need it to do.

The "Get Your Head in the Game" Manifesto

1. Burn the "Until" List: Whatever you're waiting for is a lie.

2. Stop the "Correcting" Obsession: You are a work in progress, and the Work is already in progress.

3. Move Like the Eunuch: When you hear the call, find the nearest "water" and jump in.

4. Own Your Lane: Remember Chapter 4? You can't get your head in the game if you're looking at someone else's scoreboard.

5. Use the 5 second rule to get your brain into attention

The Summer of the Spiral: When Comparison Becomes a Physical Poison

In the summer of 2024, I wasn't just in a "comparison trap"—I was in a full-blown spiritual and physical tailspin.

I had fallen for the ultimate Serpent hack: I started comparing my actual life to the fictional "should be" life. I became my own god. I thought if I just worked harder, obsessed more, and "manifested" better, I could control the outcome. I started binge-watching the wrong preachers on YouTube—the ones who tell you that you are the center of the universe, the ones who sell a gospel of self-worship disguised as "success."

Here's the neuro-spiritual math: Comparison + Self-Worship = System Failure.

Night after night, the sleep I desperately needed was stolen by the enemy's playlist. My brain was stuck in a high-beta frequency of panic. I was vibrating at such a distorted pitch that my physical hardware started to glitch.

The Midnight "Heart Attack"

One night, the feedback squeal got so loud I thought my heart was literally exploding. I was convinced it was the end.

My wife rushed me to the ER. She said I was gasping for air, clutching my chest—only to find out it was a massive panic attack. But God uses the "scares" to reveal the "secrets." Because of that panic attack, the doctors ordered a battery of tests, including a CT scan that would forever change the way I viewed my life.

That's when they found it: The Brain Tumor.

Talk about a "Get your head in the game" moment. God literally had to show me the physical manifestation of the pressure I was putting on myself. The tumor was the ultimate "Stop" sign. I spent two nights in the hospital, staring at the ceiling, realizing that my "self-god" status had failed me.

The Ireland Mistake: Running on Empty

And what did I do? Did I sit in the sanctuary and recover? No. I doubled down on the "hustle."

The very next week after being discharged, I hopped on

a plane to Ireland for work. I was terrified, I had a literal mass in my brain, and yet I was still trying to stay in the "wrong lane." I was trying to prove I was "fine," trying to keep up with the fictional version of myself I'd created.

I shouldn't have gone. I was running on the fumes of a broken ego. I was trying to play a stadium show with a broken instrument. If you're reading this and you're in your own version of "Ireland"—running away from your healing because you're afraid of looking "behind"—stop the plane.

Why You Can't Wait Until You're "Perfect"

My trip to Ireland was an attempt to make my life look "correct" while my head was literally falling apart. I was trying to complete my own work instead of letting the One who started the good work finish it.

The lesson I learned the hard way? You cannot heal in the same environment (or mindset) that made you sick. I had to get my head in the game—the real game. Not the game of "looking successful in Ireland," but the game of "surrendering to the Surgeon in the Sanctuary."

Reality Check: If you're losing sleep comparing your life to a YouTube video, you aren't just tired; you're being poisoned. Don't wait for a brain tumor diagnosis to start listening to the right frequency.

Finding your "actual" Frequency in the Sanctuary

We often spend our energy trying to "tune in" to success, or even to our own talent, but the right frequency—that specific thing God has called us to do—isn't found in the noise of the world. It is found in the sanctuary. It's found when we get on our knees and actually seek God's face rather than just His hands.

In Scripture, we see the apostle Paul struggling with a "thorn in his flesh." He pleaded with God three times to take it away, but God's response wasn't a removal of the problem; it was a revelation of His presence. God told him, "My grace is sufficient for you, for my power is made perfect in weakness." You may be in that same boat right now. You might be asking God to remove a barrier, a bit of "writer's block" in your life, or a season of dryness. But God wants to reveal Himself to you in the sanctuary first.

From Striving to Surrendering

I experienced this firsthand while working on my current 15-song album. For the longest time, I felt stuck. I couldn't find those beautiful, soul-stirring melodies to match the message in my heart. I couldn't even find the poignant lyrics necessary to express how truly awesome God is. I was trying to create rather than receive.

Then, during a 4:00 AM prayer session, God spoke to my heart: "My grace is enough. When you spend time with me, I will reveal everything you are asking for."

That shift changed everything. As I stopped focusing on the "output" and started focusing on the Outpour, the creativity began to flow. Little by little, as I found joy in simply worshipping Him for who He is, something inside me released. Melodies and lyrics began to pour out—not from my effort, but from His inspiration.

Breaking the Block

If you are facing a "writer's block" in your own life—whether in your career, your relationships, or your purpose—the solution isn't to work harder. It is to enjoy God just for who He is.

When you prioritize the sanctuary over the studio, and the Creator over the craft, you will notice your heart and mind begin to flow. His grace is the key that unlocks the frequency you've been searching for.

EDWIN SANTOS

The Anointed Vs. The Arrogant

We are officially halfway through the book. You've nailed down your sound, survived the ego-death of comparison, and found your mental "Sanctuary" button. You're looking good. You're sounding good. Now, we have to talk about how you show up.

There's a tension that exists in every arena of success—especially in the Kingdom—and it centers around authenticity. It's the tightrope walk between being confident in your anointing and being a total fraud driven by ego.

You know the critique. I've heard it, you've heard it: "Musicians have the biggest egos."

I remember reading Marcos Witt—a true pioneer in worship music—talk about this, and it totally reframed my thinking. He suggested that what people often perceive as arrogance or ego in a musician isn't always vanity. Sometimes, it's the sheer force of the Holy Spirit's power being channeled through a focused person.

Think about it: when the anointing lands, it's intense. It's a fire. It's a frequency so pure that it demands attention.

If a musician or leader owns that power and operates at that level of focused intensity, it can be misinterpreted by observers who aren't experiencing that same frequency.

The difference isn't the intensity; it's the source.

- Ego: Power derived from self-promotion, performance, and fear of failing. It's faking it.

- Anointing: Power derived from surrender, integrity, and the Holy Spirit. It's being real.

The best thing to do is to quit faking the former and start owning the latter.

The Prophet's Mic Drop

Asaph's most savage, no-filter critique came in the form of Psalm 50. This psalm is his prophetic mic drop—a message he spoke from the very heart of God's presence, telling the entire assembly to stop lying to themselves.

The people were back to their old habits. They were showing up to the Tent of Meeting, bringing their sacrifices (mostly bulls), and going through the motions. They were doing religion perfectly, but their hearts were miles away. They were faking it.

So Asaph, the Seer who sees the spiritual reality behind the physical act, drops this bomb:

"I have no need of a bull from your stall or goats from your pens, for every animal of the forest is mine, and the cattle on a thousand hills. If I were hungry, I would not tell you, for the world is mine, and all that is in it." (Psalm 50:9-12, NIV)

The message is savage: God doesn't need your stuff! He doesn't need your perfectly tuned drums, your flawlessly executed worship service, or your carefully curated Instagram picture of "blessedness." He owns everything already.

The sacrifice (the bull) was just the analogue representation of the real requirement, which is the digital truth: the human heart.

They were giving God their performance (the bull on the altar) instead of their presence (their surrendered heart). They were faking the friendship by substituting ritual for intimacy.

The Integrity Frequency

If you've ever felt exhausted in your spiritual life, it's likely because you've been working the "fake it" game.

Faking it takes astronomical energy because you are constantly trying to manage external perception.

• Faking it means you try to look happy, successful, and put-together when you're dead inside. (Me, on that drum riser, pretending I wasn't ruined by sin.)

• Being real means you walk in integrity, knowing that your internal reality matches your external representation.

Look what God asks for instead of the bull:

"Sacrifice thank offerings to God, fulfill your vows to the Most High, and call on me in the day of trouble; I will deliver you, and you will honor me." (Psalm 50:14-15, NIV, emphasis mine)

What is a thank offering? It's not a thing you buy; it's a posture of the heart.

What is calling on Him in the day of trouble? It's vulnerability and authenticity. It's admitting you can't fix it yourself (just like I had to do on that hospital bed) and surrendering the control you thought you had.

Asaph's final lesson here is simple: Integrity is your purest frequency.

When you operate in true integrity—where the person

you are in public is the person you are in private—you stop faking it. You stop worrying about what other people call "ego," because you know you are simply responding to the anointing that's on you.

Stop trying to impress God. Stop trying to impress your church, your boss, or your spouse. Just be the raw, vulnerable, broken, and redeemed person He actually called you to be. That is the only sacrifice He actually needs, and it will liberate your energy to operate in your true power.

The old temple vs. the new temple

During Asaph's time the temple was an outdoor tent that served as the place to bring sacrifices to God and atone for your sin, but then David passed away. David's son Solomon was led by God's spirit to take temple building to a whole other level. That old messy, dirty, chaotic and temporary temple had to be turned into a real stone and mortar building in which the people of Israel could come and meet with the presence of God. Let's talk about that ark that contained the most sacred possession on the face of the earth, God's presence.

The ark of the covenant

There are objects in Scripture that aren't just holy; they're terrifying. They're the cosmic VIP access pass wrapped up in a danger sign. They're mysterious, they're powerful, they're feared, and they're revered.

The Ark of the Covenant is all of those things—and then some. It's the spiritual singularity where heaven slams into earth, where noise meets silence, where glory is so close it might burn you. It's not a museum piece. It's a literal, tangible intersection of Worship and Warfare.

And no one, no one, got that terrifying intersection better than Asaph, the prophetic drummer of Israel.

The Ark wasn't some mediocre church choir instrument. It wasn't a nuclear reactor you read about in a history book. It was something infinitely more important:

The Throne of Divine Frequency.

It was the one spot on the planet where God's presence wasn't just a nice feeling; it was a measurable, tangible, holy-Lord-I-can-feel-that-in-my-guts force.

This chapter is your bridge. It's the connection between the sound of heaven, the {G.O.A.T.} status of a worship drummer, and the sacred, explosive responsibility Asaph carried with his cymbals.

1. The Ark: God's Resonant Throne (Spoiler: It's Not a Box)

When God handed Moses the blueprint for the Ark, He wasn't like, "Hey, build me a nice storage box." He was building a resonant throne—a powerhouse where His presence could chill without instantly vaporizing everything around it.

It was designed like a cosmic capacitor:

• Acacia wood: Non-conductive core. Stability.

• Gold (inside and out): Conductive layers. Purity.

• Two Cherubim: Wings forming an acoustic canopy. Visual and Sound Focus.

This wasn't some flimsy CB700 drumset. This was built for a manifestation that would make your hair stand on end. The power wasn't electrical; it was the presence of Yahweh, focused and cranked up to a thousand.

The Bible literally says, "The LORD dwelleth between the cherubims." (1 Samuel 4:4).

The Ark wasn't sometimes powerful. It was always powerful. The question wasn't, "Will God show up?" The question was, "Are you aligned enough not to be killed by it?"

The Sound Protocol: Why Music Was Non-Negotiable

The Ark was the centerpiece of David's tabernacle—a tent with no veil, no walls, no separation. God's presence was out in the open, ready to go. And what surrounded that wide-open glory?

A non-stop, 24/7, music marathon.

We're talking 4,000 musicians and 288 prophetic singers. Asaph, Heman, and Jeduthun were the bandleaders. God commanded this continuous sound, not because He needed to be entertained, but because SOUND CREATES ALIGNMENT.

- God speaks - Reality forms.

- Sound - Precedes victory.

- Sound - Shatters walls.

- Sound - Summons heaven.

- Sound - Sanctifies space.

The Ark didn't play music. It demanded it. It didn't generate rhythm. It attracted it. The Ark was the throne, and Music was the protocol.

3. The Cymbals: Not for Everyone (Only the Seer)

So, why the cymbals? And why was only Asaph allowed to touch them? You wanna know the answer? It's because the cymbals were the Prophetic Triggers. Cymbals were not rhythm toys. They were Prophetic Triggers.

The Bible is explicit: "Asaph sounded with cymbals." (1 Chronicles 16:5).

Why him? Because cymbals require the works: Timing. Discernment. Prophetic Perception. Instant Responsiveness to God.

Who better to handle the most explosive instrument than a seer-musician? Asaph's cymbals weren't about filling time; they were for Revelation.

Your Story: The musician Who Gets the Weight

If you're a worship team drummer (or know one), you know the importance of dynamics. You know that sometimes the drummer plays like a freight train, and so does everyone else, sometimes the drummer plays soft enough to hear a pin drop, and sometimes the drummer sits out entirely.

You know that the drummer is always responsible for the pulse of the room.

A worship drummer:

- Controls the rise and fall of the volume in the room.

- Anticipates the transition before the worship leader even breathes it.

- Carries the weight of the atmosphere.

- Can make a chorus explode or collapse with a single stroke.

In reality, The Drummer is the Gatekeeper of Worship Dynamics.

That is exactly what Asaph did with those cymbals.

Now let me get your attention especially if you're a drummer for this next part. You as the drummer, and Asaph share the same spiritual assignment—you just happen to have a few more pieces of hardware. Asaph wasn't just crashing away; he was:

- Timing Prophecy.

- Releasing Moments.

- Announcing Divine Shifts.

- Accenting God's Presence.

Just like you do when you bring the bridge back, swell

the toms, or set the tempo of breakthrough. Asaph used cymbals like you use your kit: Not as noise, but as Direction.

Dynamics Are Divine (God Plays Loud and Soft)

I have always told my students, "As a drummer... there are parts where you play louder, softer, and sometimes not at all."

Listen up: That is not just musical wisdom—it is Theology.

God Himself moves in dynamics:

• Loud: Thunder on Sinai. The Sound of Rushing Waters. Explosive Power.

• Soft: The Whisper to Elijah. The Gentle Leading of the Spirit. Intimate Guidance.

• Silent: When heaven tests your faith. When God lets you wrestle. Inward Transformation.

If God is dynamic, your worship must be dynamic. If God is expressive, His musicians must be expressive.

This is why your story belongs here. Because like Asaph, you learned to obey God's quiet moments and His explosive ones.

You and Asaph Share the Same Calling

You are a prophetic musician. Asaph was a seer-musician.

And just as the Ark responded to Asaph's strategic worship, your life still carries the same Asaphite assignment—to hear, to lead, to obey, and to unleash the sound that aligns hearts to God. That's why it's important to know the weight of your calling. You are not just some paid bassist that shows up on Sundays to make the music at a random church sound nice, you're a prophetic vessel that God uses in His temple.

Stop Faking the Temple

We have spent far too long treating the church building as the only place where God dwells. We put on our "Sunday best," change our vocabulary for two hours, and then leave the presence of God behind in the pews. We are faking a version of holiness that is tied to a physical address.

But when Jesus died and the veil was torn, the definition of "the temple" changed forever. It is time to quit faking that the church building is the temple and actually take up the weight of the responsibility God has placed on us.

The New Architecture

The New Testament is uncompromising about this shift. We are no longer visiting a holy place; we *are* the holy place.

- 1 Corinthians 3:16: "Don't you know that you yourselves are God's temple and that God's spirit dwells in your midst?"

- 1 Corinthians 6:19-20: "Do you not know that your bodies are temples of the Holy Spirit, who is in you, whom you have received from God? You are not your own; you were bought at a price."

This isn't a poetic metaphor; it is a spiritual reality. If you are a follower of Christ, you are carrying the Glory of the Living God into your workplace, your kitchen, your car, and your gym.

A Serious Responsibility

God takes this very seriously. In the Old Testament, the temple had to be purified and handled with absolute reverence. If we are now that temple, how are we treating ourselves?

When we "fake it"—living one way in the sanctuary and another way in the world—we are desecrating the very temple God died to establish. We cannot "turn off" our faith because we aren't "at church." You cannot leave the temple when the temple is you.

Stop playing a part. Stop pretending holiness is a destination you visit once a week. It's time to take the responsibility of being God's dwelling place seriously. Your life is the only "sanctuary" some people will ever step into. What kind of atmosphere are they finding there?

EDWIN SANTOS

The Sound Of Selective Amnesia

Look, if you've had a major spiritual breakthrough—like finding your Kingdom frequency, surviving a near-death experience, or pulling yourself out of the gutter of comparison—you have a story. That story is pure gold. It's a map. It's a blueprint.

The problem? Most people treat their spiritual victories like a great concert that only exists in the moment, a mere event. They walk off stage, pack up the gear, and forget to record the lesson.

This is a failure of legacy. You can be the most anointed, most powerful person in the room, but if you don't build a sustainable system for transferring that frequency to the next generation, you're just a flash in the pan. You're a one-hit wonder.

Asaph, the Chief Seer, saw this problem coming a mile away. His biggest contribution to the Kingdom wasn't just the songs he wrote; it was the history lesson he left behind.

Psalm 78—which Asaph wrote—is a monster of a chapter. It's one of the longest in the Bible, and it's basically an entire history lecture dedicated to one thing: You keep screwing up because you keep forgetting the miracles God did for your grandparents.

The Three-Minute Rule of Miracles

Asaph starts Psalm 78 by saying:

"My people, hear my teaching; listen to the words of my mouth... We will not hide them from their children; we will tell the next generation the praiseworthy deeds of the Lord, his power, and the wonders he has done." (Psalm 78:1, 4, NIV)

Why did he have to write this down? Because people have a spiritual attention span that is roughly three minutes long. We have the memories of goldfish when it comes to God's faithfulness.

The generation that watched the Red Sea part was the same generation that complained about having no water. The generation that saw manna rain from the sky was the same generation that worshipped a golden calf.

And guess what? You and I are no different. We get rescued from brain surgery, pulled out of the sin spiral, or lifted out of crippling depression, and within six months of smooth sailing, we start to think, "Maybe I didn't need God that much after all."

Selective amnesia is spiritual warfare. The enemy doesn't need to defeat you with massive temptation; he just needs you to *forget* the price of your freedom. He wants you to forget that disabled bed, forget that panic attack, forget the sheer grace that pulled you out.

If you forget, you stop depending. If you stop depending, you start trying to be your own god again (remember Chapter 5?). And that, my friend, is how you crash and burn.

Storytelling is Spiritual Warfare

Asaph didn't just teach the next generation how to play the cymbals (the skill); he taught them why we play (the history).

He went through the whole family photo album: the miracles in Egypt, the wilderness wandering, the discipline they endured, and the ultimate faithfulness of God. It wasn't a feel-good sermon. It was a rigorous, sometimes painful recounting of failures and redemptions.

Why?

"So the next generation would know them, even the children yet to be born, and they in turn would tell their children. Then they would put their trust in God and would not forget his deeds but would keep his commands." (Psalm 78:5-7, NIV)

The point of your story isn't just to make you feel good. It's to build trust in the future generation.

Your story is the anchor that keeps them from drifting when the storm hits. When your kids, or your mentees, or your business partners face a similar challenge, they don't need a vague piece of advice. They need your proof. They need to hear:

- "When I thought I was going to die on that operating table, God showed up."

- "When I was so deep in darkness with pornography and sin, God created a panic attack to save me."

- "When I almost quit ministry because I envied the prosperity of the wicked, God showed me their ending in the Sanctuary."

You are a conduit. If you hoard the story, the flow stops with you. (Shout out to my coach Lidia!)

Become an Asaph Ancestor

The greatest reward Asaph received wasn't the title of Chief Musician, but the fact that he founded a dynasty. Hundreds of years later, in the Bible, you still see references to the "Sons of Asaph."

That is legacy.

The Sons of Asaph weren't just guys who had the same last name; they inherited a frequency. They didn't have to start from scratch. They were born into a rhythm of prophetic worship, historical memory, and uncompromising clarity (the cymbal frequency, remember?).

They carried the torch that Asaph had lit.

This means your assignment is not complete when you find your breakthrough. It's complete when you successfully transfer that frequency to someone else.

Stop treating your wisdom as a private possession. Start seeing yourself as an ancestor—someone whose life is meant to be a historical document for the generation that follows. Don't be that guy who forgets. Tell the story, write the history, and secure the foundation so that the Sons of Asaph who follow you can be stronger, faster, and clearer than you ever were.

As musicians, teachers, and influencers, we often get caught up in our own "performance." We focus on our current album, our current class, or our current follower count. But there is a greater assignment than our own success: the *baton*. In the Kingdom of God, success without a successor is failure. We are called to be a bridge, not a dead end.

The Enemy's Tactic: Spiritual Amnesia

The enemy uses a subtle but deadly tactic in our modern world: he tries to make us forget our ancestors. He wants us to believe we are "self-made," disconnected from the faith of those who came before us, or—worse—shackled by the mistakes of our fathers.

When you don't know where you came from, you don't know the value of what you carry. As musicians, if we forget that our talent is a gift meant to be passed down, the music dies with us. We must teach the "next round" that God wants to use them just as much as He used us. The song must continue through their lives.

The Math of Blessing vs. The Math of Curses

God is very clear about the impact of generations. In the Ten Commandments (Exodus 20:5-6), we see a striking contrast:

"...punishing the children for the sin of the parents to the third and fourth generation of those who hate me, but showing love to a thousand generations of those who love me and keep my commandments."

Notice the math of God's heart. He allows the consequences of sin to linger for four generations, but He pours out blessings for a thousand. He is looking for one person in the bloodline who is willing to be the "Curse Breaker."

Breaking the Shackles

As the late Dr. Myles Munroe often taught, a generation's purpose is to provide a platform for the next. However, many of us are held back by "generational shackles"—patterns of addiction, poverty, or spiritual apathy that have been passed down.

To be a true influencer or teacher, you must first do the hard work of getting rid of those shackles. You cannot pass on a "clean" melody if your own instrument is still bound by the spirit of your ancestors' mistakes.

1. Identify the Pattern: Look at what held your parents back.

2. Repent and Renounce: Use the authority given to you by God's Spirit to say, "This stops with me."

3. Start Anew: Begin a new "thousand-generation" blessing by living in God's will.

The Teacher's Mandate

We aren't just teaching people how to play notes or speak to a crowd; we are teaching them how to carry a legacy. When we train our disciples and students, we must instill in them the responsibility to teach the person after them.

Don't be the guy who forgets that he was once a student. Don't be the guy who hoards his knowledge because he's afraid of being replaced. Be the guy who builds a foundation so strong that the next generation can stand on your shoulders and reach notes you never could.

The Living Example: The Story of Azarai

If you want to understand what it looks like to "not be the guy that forgets," you have to look at people like my friend, Azarai. For years, her mission has been clear: she is a music teacher at our church with a relentless passion for the next generation.

Every Friday, she would pour out her soul, teaching children—including my own kids from the time they were very little—the foundations of music theory and the mechanics of their instruments. But she didn't stop at the technical side. She taught them how to listen to one another in a band and, most importantly, she taught them the true heart of worship.

The harvest of her labor is undeniable. Several of her students didn't just learn a hobby; they caught the fire. Today, most of them have graduated to the Middle School and High School bands as well as the main worship band at the church, carrying the torch she lit for them.

When the Walls Close In

You would think a ministry that produces such a tangible, spiritual harvest would be protected at all costs. But sometimes, the enemy uses "unforeseen circumstances" or institutional shifts to try and silence the music.

Azarai was eventually told she could no longer use the church facilities for these lessons and rehearsals. It was a crushing blow. To have the place where you've birthed so many disciples suddenly close its doors to your calling is a pain that goes deep. Like the psalmist Asaph in Psalm 73, who said his feet had "almost slipped" when he saw the prosperity of the wicked and the injustice of his situation, Azarai felt the weight of that discouragement.

When you are doing God's work and the "system" turns against you, it's easy to want to give up. It's easy to let the "shackles" of bitterness take hold.

The God Who Provides a Way

But here is the beauty of the "thousand-generation" blessing: God never forsakes His called. Because Azarai remained faithful to the students and the sound God gave her, God didn't let the ministry die. He provided a new studio—a dedicated space where she can continue to shape these young musician-disciples without limitation.

This is the lesson for all of us: The "temple" isn't the building (as we discussed in the last chapter), and the ministry isn't the facility. The ministry is the *people*. As long as Azarai has a heart to teach and the kids have a heart to learn, the music must—and will—keep going.

Don't Let the Music Stop with You!

Azarai refused to be the one who "forgot" the next generation just because things got difficult. She understood that if she stopped, a link in the chain would break.

Ask yourself:

• Am I investing in someone who can take my place?

• Am I allowing temporary setbacks to stop a permanent calling?

- Am I building a legacy that will outlive the building I'm currently standing in?

Don't let the music die with you. Whether it's in a church hall or a small studio, keep pouring out your soul. The harvest depends on it.

The Scarcity of the Laborer

When we look at the landscape of modern ministry, we often see a lot of people who want the spotlight, but very few who want the "Friday night" grind of teaching a child how to hold a guitar pick or find middle C. Jesus looked out at the crowds and felt a deep compassion because He saw a specific problem:

"The harvest is plentiful, but the laborers are few. Therefore pray earnestly to the Lord of the harvest to send out laborers into his harvest." (Matthew 9:37-38)

Azarai is that laborer. While others are chasing "platforms," she is out in the field, hands in the dirt, planting seeds of theory and worship into young hearts. The "harvest" isn't just the people sitting in the pews; the harvest is the potential trapped inside a ten-year-old who doesn't yet know they have a song to sing. If we don't have laborers like Azarai to cultivate that talent, the harvest rots in the field.

The Asaph Moment: When the Sanctuary Becomes a Struggle

As I mentioned, Azarai's soul was crushed when the doors closed. This is a "Selah" moment—a pause where we have to ask why God allows the "laborer" to be kicked out of the field they were tending.

In Psalm 73, Asaph looked at the world and saw things that didn't make sense. He saw the proud prospering while he was struggling to be faithful. He said, "But as for me, my feet had almost slipped; I had nearly lost my foothold" (Psalm 73:2). He didn't find peace until he "entered the sanctuary of God."

For Azarai, the test was: Is your calling attached to the building, or is it attached to the Master of the Harvest? When she realized the "sanctuary" was carried inside her, she was able to step over the hurdle of rejection and move into the new space God provided.

The New Ground: A Studio Anointed for Discipleship

The fact that God provided a studio isn't just a "nice ending"—it is a divine endorsement. It is God saying, "If they won't give you a room, I'll give you a building." This new studio is more than a place for music lessons; it is a greenhouse for the next generation of Levites. In 2

Timothy 2:2, Paul tells Timothy:

"And the things you have heard me say in the presence of many witnesses entrust to reliable people who will also be qualified to teach others."

This is the "Four-Generation" rule in action. Azarai was taught, she teaches my children, and now my children are joining the main band to lead others. The studio is the place where the "generational shackles" of musical silence are broken. Every scale they practice and every chord they learn is a strike against the enemy's plan to make us forget our heritage.

The Cost of the "Yes"

To the person reading this who feels like their "field" has been taken away: Don't mistake a change in location for a change in vocation. Azarai's story teaches us that if you are a laborer for the Harvest, the Lord of the Harvest will always ensure you have a place to work. It might not look like the church basement anymore. It might look like a storefront studio, a living room, or a digital space. But as long as you refuse to be "the guy that forgets," God will provide the ground.

Who is Your Azarai?

As you close this chapter, I want you to look around your

own life. We all need to be part of a "triple-threat" cycle of legacy. To avoid being "the guy that forgets," you must ask yourself three hard questions:

1. Who is my Paul? Who is the "Azarai" in your life that you should be learning from? We never outgrow the need for a mentor. If you aren't being poured into, you will eventually run dry.

2. Who is my Timothy? Who are you currently teaching? If you have a skill—whether it's playing the piano, leading a team, or understanding the Word—you are a steward of that knowledge. You have a responsibility to find a "Friday night" student and pour into them.

3. What is my "Studio"? If the doors of the traditional "temple" have closed on you, have you stopped working, or have you looked for the new ground God is providing?

The Harvest Cannot Wait

The enemy wants you to focus on the closed door, the lack of facilities, or the politics of a building. He wants you to get stuck in the "Asaph moment" where your feet begin to slip into bitterness. But remember: The harvest is ready right now. The kids are waiting. The next generation of musicians is waiting. The "thousand-generation" blessing is waiting to be activated through your obedience. Azarai didn't need a church building to be a minister; she just needed a heart that refused to let the music stop.

Don't be the link in the chain that breaks. Be the one who remembers where the gift came from, uses it to break generational shackles, and then hands the instrument to the next person with a smile. The sound of the Kingdom depends on our willingness to stay in the field, no matter where that field happens to be.

When Polite Prayer Isn't Enough

You've got your spiritual frequency tuned, you're walking in integrity, and you're starting to pass on your story. Now, how do you sustain the fire? You pray.

But let's be real, most of us have been taught to pray polite, gentle, "churchy" prayers. We whisper vague requests: "Lord bless this food, Lord we pray you "just" bless that person, and "just" give me peace."

I am here to tell you that polite prayers are cute, but desperate prayers move mountains.

Intercession—the act of standing in the gap and fighting for an outcome—is not a passive activity for grandmas in the back room. It's a spiritual weapon for anyone who is serious about establishing God's Kingdom as Asaph and his sons did. If you want to shift the atmosphere, you can't just send up a suggestion. You have to roar at Heaven.

The Recovery Roar

I learned the difference between whispering and roaring during the two and a half months I was recovering from brain surgery.

I was physically disabled. I couldn't walk normally. I was completely reliant on help, including my mother-in-law feeding me three times a day. If you want to talk about ego-death (Chapter 6), try having someone feed you when you were just leading teams of huge strong men to build massive audio and video projects all over the world six months ago. The external glory was completely stripped away. But here is what happens when you hit rock bottom: your deepest God-given frequency is activated. When you can't physically do anything, all you can be is a desperate voice.

My prayer wasn't a gentle request. It was a fierce, daily declaration that echoed the sheer terror and the miraculous reprieve I had been given. I would pray something like this:

"Thank you, Holy Spirit, for keeping me alive. I know you have a purpose for me even after my brain surgery. You know why my brain didn't expand when I was in airplanes traveling for work. You have a purpose for me, and I will not keep missing it."

Do you hear the fire in that? That's not a wish; that's a demand of destiny. None of this "just" bless me Lord.

I wasn't asking if God had a purpose; I was declaring He

had one and I was refusing to let go until I understood it. The prayer was fueled by the stark reality of the miracle: that a tumor-filled brain hadn't exploded during atmospheric pressure changes thousands of feet in the air. That was an intentional preservation, and I was going to leverage that mercy into momentum.

That is the sound of a spiritual roar—it's gritty, it's specific, and it's fueled by a holy desperation that says, "I will not waste the second chance you gave me."

Asaph's Three-Line Intercession

Now let's look at Asaph's Psalm 80. It's a collective prayer of intercession, and it contains the most famous three-line prayer in the entire Bible:

"Restore us, O God; make your face shine on us, that we may be saved." (Psalm 80:3)

"Restore us, O God Almighty; make your face shine on us, that we may be saved." (Psalm 80:7)

"Restore us, O Lord God Almighty; make your face shine on us, that we may be saved." (Psalm 80:19)

Asaph screams this same prayer three times, increasing the intensity each time (from "O God" to "O God Almighty" to "O Lord God Almighty").

He is not being polite; he is demanding a frequency shift.

This prayer isn't saying, "Hey, if you get a chance, could you "just" maybe fix things?" It's a command backed by the confidence of a prophet.

1. Restore Us: This is the demand for Re-Tuning. "Put us back the way we were designed to be, before we broke ourselves."

2. Make Your Face Shine on Us: This is the demand for Presence. "Show up so obviously that no one can deny you are here."

3. That We May Be Saved: This is the demand for Purpose. "We need you to save us so we can complete our mission."

Asaph was using his words like spiritual crash cymbals, demanding that Heaven open up and intervene. His prayer wasn't based on how good they were; it was based on the fact that their survival was essential to God's purpose.

The Liturgy of Purpose

The most potent prayers are those that link your personal desperation to God's eternal purpose. You stop praying selfishly ("Heal me so I feel better") and start praying prophetically ("Heal me because you preserved me for a specific task, and I will not miss it").

The strength you gained little by little in recovery was fueled by that roar: the conviction that God had invested in you—literally preserving your life on an airplane—and that investment demanded a return.

Stop sending suggestions to Heaven. Go into your prayer space (your Sanctuary, Chapter 5), think about the miracle God performed to keep you alive and tuned, and then use that evidence to fuel a fierce, specific, and demanding roar.

The Kingdom doesn't just need your gratitude; it needs your grit. It needs you to pray with the confidence of someone who knows they were preserved for a greater assignment. Go on, get loud.

A Clean Vessel for the Roar

However, you cannot roar with a "clogged" spirit. To pray in a way that God has to respond, you must be a clean vessel.

Think of a brass instrument—a trumpet or a trombone. If there is debris inside the instrument, the sound is muffled, weak, and distorted. Many of us wonder why our prayers don't seem to reach the ceiling, but we are trying to "roar" while holding onto bitterness, secret sin, or generational shackles.

A deep relationship with God is the "cleaning process." When you spend time in His presence, in His temple, His Spirit acts like a fire that consumes the dross.

- It cleanses your motives.

- It purifies your heart.

- It aligns your will with His.

When a clean vessel roars, Heaven responds because the sound being produced is no longer just the sound of a human—it is the sound of the Holy Spirit groaning through us.

The Weight of the Secret

If you want to roar at heaven, you cannot have a muzzle on your soul. For a long time, I tried to lead, I tried to play, and I tried to pray while carrying the weight of hidden sin. I was a vessel with a crack in it, trying to hold the glory of God.

The turning point came when I stepped into a 12-step program at my church. There were seven of us—seven men struggling with the same cycle of sexual sin. We were all "good church guys" on the outside, but we were dying on the inside.

One of the guys, a brother I'll call Dan, shared a mantra that shattered my world and reconstructed it all at once:

"You are only as sick as your secrets."

Breaking the Silence

That phrase became my motto. I realized that my secrets were the walls keeping God's power out. When you hide a sin, you give it a dark room to grow in. You can't "roar" when you're constantly looking over your shoulder to see if someone has found you out.

Since the day I decided to become an "open book," my life has been heaven on earth. The "shackles" didn't just loosen; they fell off. Transparency didn't make me weak; it made me dangerous to the enemy. Now, when I worship or write music, there is no static on the line. I am a clean vessel.

Finding Your Person

If you are reading this and you are struggling with a hidden addiction—whether it's sexual sin, substance abuse, or deep-seated bitterness—you must find an exit ramp for your secrets.

James 5:16 says: "Therefore confess your sins to each other and pray for each other so that you may be healed."

Healing doesn't happen in isolation. It happens in the light. But here is a warning: Not everyone is qualified to hear your heart.

Don't go to your "drinking buddies" to talk about your alcohol addiction.

Don't go to your "smoking buddies" to talk about your cigarette addiction.

Ask God to guide you to a person of character—a man if you're a man, or a woman if you're a woman—who is strong enough to hold the weight of your truth without dropping it.

The Clean Vessel Roars Louder

When you empty the trash of your secrets, you create a massive space for the Holy Spirit to fill. The roar of a man or woman who has nothing left to hide is a sound that shakes the gates of hell.

Praying for the Next Generation

We don't just roar for ourselves; we roar for the "next round" we discussed in the last chapter. We roar for our students, our children, and our disciples.

The enemy wants a silent generation. He wants the music to stop. He wants the teachers to give up. When you roar at Heaven, you are clearing the spiritual atmosphere so that the next generation can breathe. You are praying in a way that breaks the resistance they would have faced.

The Response is Guaranteed

God is not intimidated by your roar. In fact, He is invited by it. When Jesus was on the cross, He cried out with a loud voice. When the blind man on the side of the road heard Jesus passing by, he didn't just speak—he shouted until he was heard.

If you are a clean vessel, and you are standing in the sanctuary of your own heart as the temple of God, your roar becomes a frequency that Heaven cannot ignore. It is the frequency of faith.

The Weight of the Seer: My Daughter's Story

As we talk about being a clean vessel for the next generation, I see this reality unfolding in my own home. My daughter is beginning to show the symptoms of a heavy calling—a counselor's heart mixed with what I believe is a brewing prophetic spirit. People are already drawn to her for advice, and God has begun speaking to her through dreams.

But the "next level" of spiritual sight isn't always filled with light and peace; sometimes, it begins with terror.

Recently, she had a dream so vivid and terrible that it left her in tears, shaken by fear and terror. As a father, it's hard to watch your child suffer, but God made me feel something profound: The visions will continue because the gift is being developed. God is preparing her for what may become an anointed ministry that brings freedom and hope to generations

From Terror to Mastery

I remember when I first started playing the drums at church. At first, it was nerve-wracking. The volume, the responsibility, and the fear of making a mistake were terrifying. I was scared to hit the skins. But as I stayed consistent, that fear transformed into reverence. I learned how to respect the music, the flow of the church, and the other musicians.

What started as terror ended as a disciplined, powerful gift.

My daughter is in that "nerve-wracking" stage of her spiritual gift. She is a modern-day seer in training. To help people get closer to God, she has to be able to see the things that others miss—and sometimes, that includes seeing the darkness that needs to be overcome.

The Asaph Struggle: Entering the Sanctuary

Like Asaph, whose feet almost slipped because of the weight of what he saw in the world, my daughter is learning that the only way to handle the "terror" of the vision is to get closer to God.

"When I tried to understand all this, it troubled me deeply till I entered the sanctuary of God..." (Psalm 73:16-17)

For her, and for anyone God is calling to a higher level of discernment, getting close to God is imperative. You cannot handle a prophetic weight with a shallow relationship. The "roar" in this chapter is for her, too. It's for the young counselors and seers who are being woken up at night by the Spirit.

The Slow Burn of the Calling

We often want the gift without the process. We want the "seer" status without the "scary" dreams. But the next level often comes slowly, and it often requires us to walk through moments of fear so that we learn to lean entirely on His strength. Only a relationship, a deep heavily rooted relationship with God can ensure that your foot will not slip.

The Heritage of the Long Haul: The Sons of Asaph

When we talk about the "slow burn" of my daughter's gift, we are seeing a biblical pattern. We often think of Asaph as a solo act, but the Bible repeatedly mentions the "Sons of Asaph." These weren't just his biological children; they were a guild of musicians and seers who carried his mantle for hundreds of years.

Think about the patience required for that. When the First Temple was destroyed and the people were exiled to Babylon, the music stopped. For seventy years, the harps were hung on the willow trees. But the "Sons of Asaph" didn't lose their identity in the silence. They kept the "burn" alive in their hearts.

When they finally returned to Jerusalem to rebuild the temple (Ezra 3:10), who was standing there with cymbals in their hands, ready to roar at heaven? The Sons of Asaph. They had waited decades for that moment. Their calling wasn't a sprint; it was a 400-year marathon.

David and the Cave of Adullam

If you want to see the "slow burn" in its most terrifying form, look at David. He was anointed to be King when he was just a boy—a beautiful, high-frequency moment of "The Sanctuary." But immediately after that, he didn't go to a throne; he went to a cave.

David spent years running for his life from Saul. He lived in the "terror" of the wilderness. He had the "seer" gift—he could see the crown God promised him—but his reality was dirt, fear, and cold nights in the Cave of Adullam.

Why the delay? Because God was developing his "roar." If David had stepped onto the throne the day after he was anointed, he wouldn't have had the character to stay there. The "slow burn" of the wilderness turned a shepherd boy into a King. The terror of the cave taught him that God was his only true sanctuary.

The Training of the Seer

Just like my daughter is feeling the weight of her dreams now, and just like I felt the "nerves" of the drum throne, the Bible shows us that God never rushes a masterpiece.

• Moses had a 40-year "slow burn" in the desert before the burning bush.

• Paul spent three years in Arabia after his Damascus Road encounter before he began his true ministry.

• Asaph's sons practiced in the shadows of exile so they could lead the roar of the restoration.

The terror my daughter feels isn't a sign that she's failing;

it's a sign that the gift is heavy. In the physical world, if you pick up a heavy weight too fast, you'll break your back. In the spiritual world, if God gives you the "next level" before you've been through the "slow burn," the weight of the glory will crush you.

Respecting the Process

Asaph's sons had to respect the music enough to wait for the temple to be rebuilt. David had to respect the calling enough to wait for the cave to end. I have to respect my daughter's process enough to let God develop her at His pace.

The "slow burn" is where the hidden sin is burned away. It's where the "secrets" are confessed and the vessel is scrubbed clean. Don't be afraid of the time it takes. The longer the burn, the brighter the light when the roar finally breaks through. If you are a parent, an influencer, or a teacher, you must roar at heaven for these young vessels. We must pray that their terror turns into respect for the gift, and that they become clean conduits for the voice and the establishment of the kingdom of God upon the hearts of all men and women.

CHAPTER 9
SINGING WHILE THE SHIP SINKS

The Ultimate Test Of A Sound Guy

You want to know the difference between a rookie sound guy and a true professional?

The rookie shines when the gear is perfect, the power is steady, and the band plays at a decent volume. The professional? The professional shines when the house lights go out and his amplifier blows a fuse.

The ultimate test of a sound guy isn't when everything is labeled and powered; it's when the power surge takes out the board, the guitar player snaps a string, and you have to restore sound based on muscle memory, raw instinct, and feel. That's when the pressure is real, and the whole show relies on your ability to restore the frequencies in the middle of the chaos.

Resilience is not about avoiding the sinking ship; it's about finding a song—a pure frequency—to sing while you're going down.

When God's House Burns Down

Asaph was a man who saw both glory and ruin. He

was the one who celebrated the establishment of God's presence in the new, open Tent of Meeting (Chapter 2). He was a visionary who saw the eternal plan (Chapter 5).

But the Sons of Asaph, the legacy he left behind, eventually faced the unthinkable: the Temple was destroyed. Jerusalem was captured, and the symbol of God's presence on Earth—the glorious, beautiful, permanent system—was set on fire.

Imagine your entire life's work, your ministry headquarters, the one place you thought was untouchable, reduced to smoke and rubble. This is the subject of Psalms 74 and 79. These aren't songs of victory; they are songs of utter devastation.

"Your enemies have destroyed the sanctuary... Your foes have roared in the place where you met with us; they have set up their banners as signs." (Psalm 74:7, 4, NIV)

The place where they once heard the pure, prophetic frequency was now filled with the roar of the enemy. The very foundation of their faith—the physical anchor of their Kingdom frequency—was gone.

What is the natural, human response to this kind of loss? Silence. You panic, you grieve, you shut down, and you let the roar of the fire become the only sound. The spirit gets quiet, and the flesh takes over.

But Asaph's legacy didn't shut down. The Sons of Asaph didn't drop their instruments and weep quietly (not for long, anyway). They did the one thing that separates the resilient from the defeated: they wrote a Psalm in the ruins.

Your Frequency is Independent of Circumstance

This is the non-negotiable lesson of resilience: The Kingdom frequency you are tuned to must be independent of your circumstances.

If your joy only works when the drums are tuned and the lights are working, your frequency is analogue— dependent on external factors. But if your song persists when the bank account is empty, the diagnosis is bad, and the environment is hostile, your frequency is divine —dependent only on the King.

Asaph's Psalms in the ruins were not about what they had lost; they were about what God had not lost.

They cried out:

• "We know we messed up, but remember your Covenant!" (Chapter 7 in action—leveraging God's history.)

• "Don't let the enemy slander your name!" (Shifting the

focus from their pain to God's reputation.)

• "Arise, O God, and defend your cause!" (Demanding intervention from Heaven—Chapter 8 in action.)

This isn't just grief work; it's a strategic act of prophetic sound creation. They created a sound so loud, so intentional, that it demanded the spiritual atmosphere shift, even though the physical atmosphere was filled with smoke.

The Sound in Your Shipwreck

We all face shipwrecks. It might not be a national temple burning, but it's the job loss that felt like your entire identity was destroyed. It's the relationship that imploded, leaving you wandering in the wilderness. It's the chronic illness that becomes the static in your daily life, the negative report from the doctor's office that tells you that you're in stage 3 of skin cancer.

In these moments, your internal frequency needs to be louder than the external noise.

It's easy to sing when you're winning. It takes a "tough cookie"—a seasoned warrior—to sing when the ship is sinking.

The Winter of 2018: The Ultimate Storm

My wife is the strongest woman I know. She had already survived a lifetime of trauma—she was an abused single mother who had been through hell and back, and as the saying goes, she went back to hell just to get the keys she forgot. She is a survivor by nature.

But in the winter of 2018, a new storm hit. She was diagnosed with Stage 3 skin cancer.

These were the darkest days our family had ever seen. While I was traveling more than ever for work, she was at home facing the reality of her own mortality. She wasn't just planning her next week; she was preparing her last will and testament. When the ship of your health begins to take on water like that, the natural response is to panic. But that is where the "roar" we talked about in the last chapter meets the "song" of this one.

The Sound of the Miracle

Imagine the scene: the weight of a cancer diagnosis, the loneliness of a husband on the road, and the shadow of death looming in the room. In that space, you have to decide: Will I let the water drown my voice, or will I sing until the Great Physician shows up?

God performed a miracle in her life. It wasn't just a

medical recovery; it was a divine intervention. Today, to the glory of God, she is seven years cancer-free.

She didn't get those seven years by being quiet. She got them by refusing to let the "sinking ship" dictate her melody. Like Paul and Silas in the midnight hour of the prison, she found a way to praise God when her hands were bound by a diagnosis.

I mentioned she went back to hell to get the keys she forgot. In the Kingdom, your "keys" are your authority. Sometimes, God allows us to walk through a fiery trial—like Stage 3 cancer—not to punish us, but because there is a "key" of authority in that fire that we can't get anywhere else.

- You get the key of Healing when you've faced sickness.

- You get the key of Peace when you've faced terror.

- You get the key of Hope when you've faced a "last will and testament" moment.

Now, when she speaks to other women or when we worship together, she isn't just "faking it." She is using the keys she fought for. She is a living testimony that you can be sinking and singing at the very same time.

The Asaph Perspective: Still Standing

Asaph wrote in Psalm 73 about how his flesh and heart might fail, but God is the strength of his heart and his portion forever. My wife lived that verse. When her flesh was failing in 2018, God became her portion.

If your ship is sinking right now—if you are looking at a diagnosis, a broken bank account, or a failing relationship—don't stop the music. The song is what keeps your head above the water. The song is what summons the miracle.

I had my big test on the operating table, but I've had smaller, relentless tests since: the times when the ministry felt empty, when the tours dried up, when I doubted my calling again. In those moments, I had to stop listening to the news headlines or the internal lie that I was forgotten. I had to activate my Sanctuary Shift (Chapter 5).

The song you write in the ruins is the foundation of the reconstruction. That means:

1. Don't Go Silent: The first move of the enemy is to silence you. If you can't shout, whisper. If you can't whisper, journal. But maintain a stream of consciousness directed at God.

2. Focus on His Reputation: Stop whining about what you lack, and start demanding that God's name be glorified in your mess. "God, I don't see a way out, but you are the God of the breakthrough. Do it for your glory!"

3. Find the Rhythm of Endurance: Resilience is not a single, heroic drum solo; it's the steady, unwavering beat of the high-hat—day after day, showing up, even when you feel like quitting.

The Authority of the Word

When my wife was facing that cancer diagnosis in 2018, it felt like the waves were crashing over the sides of our lives. It felt like the ship was finally going down. It reminds me of the time the apostles were caught in a massive storm on the Sea of Galilee. These weren't amateurs; these were seasoned fishermen, and even they were terrified that they were about to drown.

They woke Jesus up in a panic, and the Bible records His response:

"He got up, rebuked the wind and said to the waves, 'Quiet! Be still!' Then the wind died down and it was completely calm." (Mark 4:39)

Peace, Be Still. I get chills every time I read that.

Notice that Jesus didn't argue with the wind. He didn't negotiate with the waves. He spoke with the authority of the One who created the water in the first place.

When you are "singing while your ship is sinking," you aren't just making noise to distract yourself from the fear. You are aligning your voice with the Voice that says, "Peace, be still." In 2018, the "wind" was Stage 3 cancer. The "waves" were the last will and testament and the dark winter nights. But when we took our "roar" to the sanctuary, the Lord spoke over my wife's body. He rebuked the cell growth. He silenced the spirit of fear. And just like that boat on Galilee, the storm eventually had to bow to the Master.

You Are Not Sinking Alone

If you feel like the storm in your life is too loud to sing over, remember this: Jesus is in the boat. He isn't watching from the shore, cheering you on from a distance. He is right there in the middle of the spray and the wind.

He is waiting for you to realize that you carry His authority. When you worship in the middle of a crisis, you are essentially telling the storm, "You might be loud, but my God is louder.' My wife is cancer-free today because the Word of God spoke "Peace" over her life. Your ship isn't going down because the Captain of the host is standing on your deck. Don't stop singing. The calm is coming.

Your life is not defined by the shipwreck; it is defined by the song you choose to sing while the ship sinks. That song—that pure, unwavering frequency—is the sign that you haven't been defeated, and it is the sound that summons your rescue.

The Faulty Sensor: A Tale of Two Storms

While my wife was facing a very real, physical storm in 2018, I experienced a different kind of "sinking ship" a few years later. I was on a flight coming into JFK Airport, looking forward to getting home from an overseas fight from Europe, when the pilot's voice came over the intercom—not with the usual landing announcement, but with a chilling instruction: "We are going to make an emergency landing."

The atmosphere in that cabin shifted instantly. We were told there was a malfunction with the landing gear. In my mind, the ship was already sinking. I was paralyzed by the thought, OMG, I'm going to die. I started praying for forgiveness for everything I'd ever done. I pulled out my phone, fingers trembling, getting ready to send a final text to my wife about where to find the life insurance policy. It was traumatic. When we finally hit the tarmac,

I looked out the window and saw a fleet of fire trucks and emergency vehicles racing alongside us, lights flashing, prepared for a disaster.

The Nothing Burger

But then, the plane slowed down. We didn't crash. We didn't slide. We just... stopped.

The technicians later discovered that the landing gear was perfectly fine. It had deployed exactly as it should have. The problem? A sensor was not calibrated correctly. It sent a "wrong signal" to the cockpit, telling the pilot the gear was up when it was actually down. There was nothing wrong with the plane at all. It was a "nothing burger" that had been dressed up like a death sentence.

Calibrating Your Spirit

How many times has your mind played that same trick on you? How many times has a small problem—a weird look from a boss, a late bill, or a minor disagreement—become a life-or-death situation in your head?

We often live in a state of terror because our "God Spirit Sensor" isn't calibrated correctly. When we aren't in prayer, when we aren't in the sanctuary, our internal sensors start sending "wrong signals."

- The sensor says: "You're going to fail." * The sensor says: "God has forsaken you." * The sensor says: "The ship is sinking."

But the truth is, the "landing gear" of God's grace is already deployed. He has already gone before you. He has already provided the Way. You are experiencing the trauma of a crash that isn't actually happening because you've lost the frequency of the Holy Spirit.

Singing Through the Signal

The difference between a "nothing burger" and a miracle often comes down to your prayer life. When you are in constant communication with the Tower—with Heaven—you can look at a flashing red light on your dashboard and say, "I hear the alarm, but I know my Pilot." Don't let a faulty sensor steal your song. Whether the storm is a real Stage 3 battle or just a miscalibrated thought, the answer is the same: Get on your knees, recalibrate your spirit in the sanctuary, and keep singing. Because when your sensor is tuned to God's truth, you'll realize that even when the fire trucks are circling, you're going to land just fine.

The Battles

There are battles in the Bible that shake mountains with thunder, trumpets, and crashing cymbals. There are also battles that happen in silence—internal wars that don't make a sound in the natural but roar in the spirit. What I learned is that God fights in both realms, and sometimes the loudest warfare is the kind no one else can hear.

The story of King Jehoshaphat is one of the loud ones. Israel was surrounded by multiple nations—Ammon, Moab, and the people of Mount Seir—a coalition so big it looked impossible to defeat. But God didn't tell them to sharpen their swords. He didn't tell them to strategize. He didn't send the generals or the captains to the front lines.

He sent the musicians.

Let's be real: I am absolutely dumbfounded by this.

When I think *"musician"*, I don't exactly think *Navy SEAL*. I think of the guy crashing on my couch who wakes up at noon and considers reheating last night's pizza a major accomplishment. I think of the slackers. The riff-raff. The artsy types who can hold a note beautifully but would probably faint if asked to hold a sword or a gun.

These guys are not exactly known for their intimidating physical prowess.

We're not talking about the vertical leap of Shaq or the bicep circumference of The Rock. We're talking about the band geeks. The drama kids. The ones who wore black before it was cool and owned more feelings than dumbbells. The ones who can explain a chord progression but might need a minute to explain how football works.

And *these* are the people God sends to the front lines?

On paper, this feels like a cosmic joke.

If you were assembling an army, you wouldn't start with the people who argue about reverb tails and lighting temperature. You wouldn't draft the ones who feel things deeply, cry during movie soundtracks, and can't find their keys because they were distracted by a melody that "came out of nowhere."

You'd want tanks. Warriors. Commandos.
Not poets with calluses on their fingers instead of their fists.

And yet—over and over again—*these* are the ones God chooses.

Not because they look strong.

But because they *hear* what others don't.

See, artists may not intimidate in the natural, but they absolutely wreck things in the unseen. They don't overpower environments—they shift atmospheres. They don't dominate rooms—they tune them. They don't charge forward with brute force—they step in and change the frequency of the entire battlefield.

That's not weakness.
That's a different kind of weapon.

The artist is trained in something most soldiers aren't: sensitivity. Timing. Discernment. The ability to listen before acting. The ability to feel what's off, even when everything looks fine. The courage to stand exposed, vulnerable, and unarmored—because creativity requires risk, and risk builds a kind of resilience you can't bench-press.

God didn't put musicians on the front lines because He ran out of warriors.

He put them there because battles aren't only won with muscle.
Some are won with sound.
Some with timing.
Some by striking the invisible first.

So yeah—on the outside, they look like the least likely candidates.

But God's Kingdom has always worked this way: flipping the script, redefining strength, and choosing the ones everyone else overlooked… to lead the charge.

Asaph's sons were to take the lead to charge against the enemy. It was an Asaphite, Jahaziel, upon whom the Spirit of the Lord fell. He released the prophecy that shaped the entire battle.

Then the singers went ahead of the army, praising God with the simple line:

"Give thanks to the Lord, for His mercy endures forever."

A sentence so simple it sounds almost naive. And yet, heaven treated it like a nuclear detonation. The singers struck the first blow—not with swords, but with sound—and the battle was decided before a single soldier lifted his shield.

> "When they began to sing, the Lord Himself set ambushes among the enemies. The nations that came to destroy Israel turned their swords on one another. Not a single Israelite soldier lifted a blade. Victory came through frequency, not force. Through worship,

not warfare." 2 Chronicles 20:22

But there are other battles—quiet ones—where the war is fought inside your chest. Battles where you don't have an army, you don't have a choir, and you don't have the sons of Asaph singing on your behalf. You just have God… and the truth He is asking you to face. I went through one of those battles.

The toughest internal battle

A season where it felt like every nation was rising up against me—not literal nations, but pressures from every side. My marriage was on the rocks because of my own decisions, choices I made while traveling that broke the trust of the woman I love. I carried guilt like a stone tied around my heart, dragging me deeper every day.

And then God gave me a vision.

A message so clear that it branded itself into my spirit:

"Confess or die."

At first it sounded harsh, almost like judgment. But looking back, it was mercy. It was God warning me that the war inside me was spiritual, emotional, and physical all at once.

Three days later, a neurologist told me I had a mass in my head that could kill me.

Three days after the vision.

Three days after God said: "Confess or die."

In that moment, I felt like Israel surrounded by enemies. My mistake, my shame, my fear, my marriage, my health—everything seemed to be collapsing on me at once. But unlike Jehoshaphat, my battle didn't start with cymbals or trumpets.

My battle started with quiet confession. Confession was my song. Honesty was my frequency. Truth was my Asaphite weapon.

It felt like the most humiliating thing I have ever done. I felt like the worst piece of trash in the world—days and months of heaviness, guilt, and self-disgust. But the Lord had already made His verdict:

"You cannot heal what you refuse to expose."

Israel had to march out singing before God delivered them.

I had to confess before God healed me.

Their battle was loud.

Mine was spiritually loud.

But God was in control of both.

Preparing for the inevitable battle

Let's visit the battle field that Asaph's sons and grandsons were raised and prepared to face (thanks to Asaph's seer prophetic vision), a massive victory orchestrated by the living God. The mood in the war room—let's call it the Crisis Huddle, because that's what it was—a pure, unfiltered panic. The air was so thick with drama and conspiracy, you could choke on it. Look, we're talking about a three-nation, all-out, "we hate you and want you wiped off the map" coalition. Moab, Ammon, Tyre—the whole darn enemy neighborhood was showing up to the party uninvited.

Jahaziel, the King's go-to guy for all things high-vibration and divine strategy, was nursing his drum in the corner. He wasn't there to count arrows; he was there because the King knew the real battlefield isn't made of dirt and chariots—it's made of energy and belief.

Then General Amram, the Voice of Limiting Beliefs, starts doing his thing, slamming his fist on the map like a true fear-monger. "Silence? You think we can pray them into silence, Asaph? They're practically shouting their death threats from the hills! They're done whispering! Their mantra is loud and clear: 'Let's wipe Israel out! Don't let their name be remembered!' We need swords, not some woo-woo song!"

Everyone was busy counting physical threats, measuring distance, and planning retreats—the classic, small-picture, I-can-only-handle-what-I-can-see approach.

Jahaziel waited. You know that moment when everyone is spinning out, and you realize you have to be the one to grab the cosmic steering wheel? That was Jahaziel. He let their chaotic frequency drop until all eyes were on him, the man who knew how to tune into the divine satellite radio.

"You're focused on the hand of the enemy," Jahaziel said, his voice dropping the mic on the whole argument. "But the hand doesn't move unless the mouth commands it. That noise you hear? That boast, that clamor? That's not just talk. That is their entire power source. Their arrogance is their strategy."

He moved to the center. His drum wasn't a cozy instrument anymore; it was a weapon of mass conviction. He wasn't praying for help; he was activating his authority. He started channeling the cosmic counter-force, echoing the boundary-setting declaration that would one day become his signature jam (Psalm 83, baby).

"They are united in their arrogance," Jahaziel boomed, pointing his finger right through the map and into the unseen spiritual space where the conspiracy was hatched. "They've consulted together and they've formed a confederacy. But their consent is a lie, their counsel is a crumbling façade, and their vibration is too low to sustain itself!"

He stamped his foot—a seismic command, not just a stomp.

"I am pulling the plug on your entire operation! I command the low-frequency counsel of confusion to cease! I charge the spirit of arrogance to mute its voice! You—spirit of destruction, you—mastermind of war—SHUT UP, ENEMY! Your boast is officially cancelled, your flimsy strategy is exposed, and your temporary unity is hereby cursed to dust!"

Holy smokes.

The spiritual atmosphere hit the physical realm so hard that a ceramic pitcher on the table didn't just crash—it imploded with a sound like a bad, muffled snare drum that just had its head rip. Outside, the wind screamed, not a natural breeze, but a violent, whipping force that ripped through the trees and instantly killed all the nervous chatter.

Amram, the general, sat paralyzed. He just watched Jahaziel place a cosmic muzzle on a three-nation threat without even drawing a dagger. The battle was over the moment Jahaziel set that non-negotiable boundary. The silence that followed wasn't emptiness; it was the sound of destiny being reset. Now, they just had to wait and see what kind of magnificent, confusing chaos this divine mic-drop would cause.

And just like Israel, God dismantled my enemies in ways I could never have orchestrated. He began healing my marriage. He guided doctors to the source of the mass. He walked with me through the valley where death was a real possibility. He showed me that spiritual warfare doesn't always look like cymbals crashing or thunder roaring.

Sometimes the loudest miracle happens in the quiet obedience of telling the truth.

Asaph's legacy teaches us something profound:

- Some victories come through sound

- Some victories come through silence

- But both come through obedience

The sons of Asaph defeated nations with praise. I defeated death, shame, and destruction with confession and worship.

Same God.

Same frequency of truth.

Different battlefield.

You have to realize that the God of Asaph still fights for His people.

Because your voice—whether singing, praying, confessing, or crying—is a weapon in the hands of the Almighty.

Because battles are not won by noise, but by surrender. Sometimes God sends a choir. Sometimes He sends a vision. Sometimes He sends a neurologist. But He always sends deliverance. The battle is the Lord's. And He is still in control.

The Audacity of the Quiet

We've been conditioned to think that worship requires a dim room, a $2,000 guitar, and a bridge that repeats sixteen times until we feel a goosebump. And listen, I love a good bridge. But if your worship stops when the chords fade out, you aren't worshiping; you're just enjoying a concert.

The deepest, most "holy-crap-did-that-just-happen" kind of worship isn't found in a melody. It's found in a choice. It's found in the moment you decide to shut your mouth, stop your frantic pacing, and actually obey the crazy thing God is whispering to your spirit. Real worship is obedience. And obedience? Well, that requires you to actually know the voice of the One giving the orders.

Take my guy Jahaziel that I was just referring to in the battle with the 3 nations. They are staring down three armies. If this were a movie, the score would be terrifying. But instead of calling a war council, they hold a prayer meeting.

Jahaziel wasn't the guy with the biggest sword. He was a Levite—a lineage of people who knew how to stay in the Presence. While everyone else was hyperventilating about their impending doom, Jahaziel was tuned into a different frequency.

How did he discern God's voice in the middle of a national panic attack?

1. He knew the Sound of the Secret Place: Jahaziel was a descendant of Asaph. He came from a family of "stayers" and "seers." He didn't have to learn God's voice while the enemy was at the gate because he had been listening to it while the sun was shining. Mic drop: You can't expect to hear God's roar in the storm if you've been ignoring His whisper in the calm.

2. He filtered out the Static: To hear God, Jahaziel had to "Shut Up." He had to ignore the sound of sharpening swords and the literal screams of fear around him. He tuned out the "facts" to hear the "Truth."

3. He delivered the "Ridiculous" Instruction: God told him to tell the King: "Don't fight. Just show up." If Jahaziel had been listening to his own ego, he would have suggested a tactical flank or a strategic retreat. But he knew it was God because the instruction made zero sense to his flesh.

Worshiping at the Edge of the Grave

When I had to face death and beat it, I didn't do it by singing a catchy chorus. I did it because I had to get "Jahaziel-level" quiet.

When death is knocking on your door, it's loud. It's rude.

It wants to be the only thing you hear. It says, "This is the end. Pack it up. You lost." But when you "Shut Up and Worship," you're telling death that it doesn't have the floor anymore. You're telling your fear to take a seat in the back row because the King is speaking. My obedience wasn't some grand, poetic gesture. It was the gritty, sweaty, terrifying act of saying "Yes" to God when my bank account, my body, and my brain were all screaming "No."

Obedience is the highest form of worship because it costs you something more than breath—it costs you your control.

CHAPTER 11

BUILDING SOMETHING THAT OUTLIVES YOU

The Vibe Check: Are You A Star Or A System?

Okay, let's get real. You're a total rock star. You've activated your authority, you're rocking your unique sound, and you've finally figured out that your problems are just an illusion from a God's-eye view. So you're winning. Now what?

The great spiritual trap is building a spectacular life, career, or ministry that relies entirely on your charisma, your energy, and your personality. You become the superstar, the bottleneck, the irreplaceable genius. And then, the second you take a vacation, burn out, or—gasp—move on to the next dimension, the whole damn thing collapses.

Why? Because you built an island instead of a continent. You built a beautiful performance for your ego, not a robust, duplicatable frequency for the Kingdom.

This isn't about being famous; it's about being eternal. If you want your sound to truly shift the atmosphere, you have to build something that doesn't crumble the second your name tag is removed from the door. You are not just a person on a mission; you are an ancestor. Start acting like it.

Asaph's Retirement Plan (Spoiler: It Worked)

We've been focusing on Asaph the individual: the Seer, the warrior, the Psalmist. But the deepest truth about his life isn't found in his own biography. It's found in the history books written centuries after he was gone.

Look at the record. When the Jewish people finally returned to Jerusalem after seventy years of Babylonian exile—a massive, world-altering reset—and they started rebuilding the broken, dusty Temple, who was there to start the worship?

"The sons of Asaph, the gatekeepers, and the Nethinim..." (Ezra 2:41)

Later, during major spiritual revivals under Kings like Josiah and Hezekiah, who was providing the prophetic direction and the music? The Sons of Asaph.

Asaph the man was dust, but the frequency he established was so powerful, the culture he imprinted was so precise, and the system he built was so robust that his spiritual DNA was still running the Temple hundreds of years later.

He didn't just train replacements; he created a lineage. He built a school of sound, a blueprint for operating in the prophetic, that outlived empires. That, my friends, is true legacy. He became an ancestor.

The Lesson: How to Build Your Immortal System

You want to stop being an island and start being an ancestor? You need to commit to two things: duplication and DNA.

1. Commit to Duplication

Most people in leadership or business are great at delegation. They hand off tasks they hate so they can focus on tasks they love. This keeps the work moving, but it keeps you in charge forever.

Asaph committed to duplication. This means training someone not just to do the task, but to carry the spirit, authority, and culture behind the task.

The shift: Stop asking, "Who can help me with this?" and start asking, "Who can run this better than me one day?"

If you feel too busy to train someone, it means you've prioritized short-term production over long-term immortality. Your ego loves being the only one who can do the job, but your legacy hates it. Start training your genius out of yourself.

2. Define Your Kingdom DNA

What was the DNA of the Sons of Asaph? It wasn't just "play music." It was: Prophetic Authority and Uncompromising Worship.

They didn't just read the Psalms their ancestor wrote; they learned how to write new ones in the midst of a crisis (like the one we saw in Chapter 10). They didn't just sing songs; they operated in the Seer realm, carrying the divine frequency.

Your legacy isn't your product, your title, or your bank account. Your legacy is the operating philosophy you pass on.

• If you run a business: What is the uncompromising value (integrity, service, innovation) that defines the DNA of your company?

• If you raise a family: What is the core frequency (faith, curiosity, love) that your children will carry?

• If you lead a team: What is the standard of excellence that stays even when you leave the room?

You must make that DNA clear, repeatable, and non-negotiable.

Don't be afraid to put your trust in the next generation. Asaph built the framework, then he trusted the frequency to guide his descendants. Stop micromanaging the future, and start mentoring your legacy now.

Asaph Didn't Fight the Battle—He Built the Battlefield

When we read the story, it's easy to imagine Asaph facing a massive, personal showdown—some climactic moment where *he* had to rise, swing, and survive. But that's not actually what happened.

Asaph didn't have a huge battle on his hands.

He had a **long obedience** on his hands.

His war wasn't fought in a single afternoon. It was fought in years of faithfulness, repetition, discipline, and devotion. While others trained their arms, Asaph trained his *spirit*. While others sharpened blades, he sharpened *discernment*. While kings planned strategies, Asaph cultivated *sound*.

And when the moment came—when the threat was real, the enemy loud, and the future uncertain—Asaph himself didn't step forward to fight.

His *training* did.

His *spirit* did.

His *legacy* did.

Through Jahaziel.

The Prophetic Isn't Improvised—It's Inherited

Jahaziel didn't wake up one morning and decide to be bold.

What came out of his mouth in that assembly wasn't spontaneous courage—it was **stored faith**. He spoke because someone before him had lived in such a way that faith became normal, not heroic.

That someone was Asaph.

Every cymbal crash, every rehearsal, every moment of worship when no one was watching—none of it was wasted. Asaph wasn't just leading songs; he was **programming a generation**. He was shaping how the next generation would hear God, respond to pressure, and interpret fear.

So when Jahaziel spoke, it wasn't a fluke.

It was fruit.

Asaph's faithfulness gave Jahaziel permission to be

faithful under pressure. His consistency created a vocabulary of trust that Jahaziel could draw from in crisis. The prophecy didn't appear out of thin air—it traveled through bloodlines, mentorship, atmosphere, and example.

This is how God works.

He rarely skips generations.
He **invests** in them.

Legacy Is the Real Battlefield

Here's the uncomfortable truth:
Most of us want *breakthrough* without *buildup*.

We want the Jahaziel moment without the Asaph life.

But the Kingdom doesn't operate on shortcuts—it operates on **continuity**.

Asaph understood something we often miss: the greatest miracles aren't always the ones you witness personally. Some of the most powerful victories you'll ever participate in will happen through people who carry *your spirit* long after you're gone.

That's not loss.

That's multiplication.

Asaph didn't lose relevance when Jahaziel stepped forward. He **won legacy**.

Why This Should Make You Want to Multiply

This is where it gets personal—and maybe a little uncomfortable.

Because when you really understand this, it does something dangerous:
It makes you want your life to continue beyond you.

Not as an ego.
As stewardship.

This is why marriage exists in God's design. Not merely for companionship, romance, or stability—but for **continuation**. For the transmission of faith, vision, courage, and sound. For the handoff of unfinished assignments to a generation capable of finishing them louder, stronger, and further than we ever could.

Children aren't a distraction from purpose.

They're how purpose **survives time**.

And this isn't just biological—it's spiritual. Whether through sons and daughters, mentorship, discipleship, or creative lineage, the call is the same: *don't let the story end with you.*

The Next Generation Is Supposed to Do More Than You

If this idea threatens you, you've misunderstood legacy. The goal was never for Asaph to be the peak.

The goal was for Jahaziel to stand on his shoulders.

God's design has always been escalation, not preservation. Increase, not nostalgia. Continuation, not control. The next generation isn't meant to admire what you did—they're meant to **outgrow it**.

Your ceiling is supposed to become their floor.

That's not failure.
That's success.

You Are Training Someone You Haven't Met Yet

Even now.

Every act of faithfulness.
Every unseen rehearsal.
Every quiet yes.
Every disciplined no.

It's all training someone—maybe a child, maybe a

spiritual son or daughter, maybe an artist who will never know your name but will carry your frequency.

Asaph didn't need to fight the battle because he had already won something far greater:

He had **prepared a successor**.

And when that successor opened his mouth, heaven moved, armies scattered, and history shifted.

That's the kind of legacy worth living for.

The Ultimate "Hold My Wine" Moment

Imagine you're Jesus. You've spent three years turning water into a nice Pinot Noir (wine), walking on oceans like they're paved sidewalks, and literally pulling people back from the Great Beyond. You're about to head out, and instead of saying, "Good luck topping that," you look at your ragtag group of friends and say:

"Actually, you're going to do way cooler stuff than I did."

That is the most incredible mic drop in the history of the universe. Jesus didn't just leave a legacy; he handed over the keys to the Ferrari and told us to go faster.

1. Own Your "Greater"

Most of us spend our lives playing small because we think it's "humble." We shrink ourselves until we're the size of a postage stamp, thinking that's what a "good person" does.

Newsflash: Playing small is actually kind of an insult to the Lord.

When Jesus said we'd do "greater things," he wasn't being metaphorical. He was acknowledging that while he was one guy in one dusty corner of the world, we are a global army of creators, healers, and world-shakers. If the guy who invented the miracle is telling you that you've got even bigger magic up your sleeve, who are you to disagree?

2. Legacy Isn't a Statue (It's an Infection)

We tend to think of legacy as a bronze bust of our own heads sitting in a park somewhere. Boring.

Jesus' legacy is 2,000 years old and it still has the power to raise the dead—not just physical bodies, but dead dreams, dead spirits, and dead hopes. Why? Because he didn't build a monument; he started a movement.

- A monument just sits there getting pooped on by pigeons.

- A movement is a frequency. It's a vibe. It's a wildfire that doesn't need the original match to keep burning.

3. Stop Worrying About the "How" and Focus on the "Relationship"

Building something that outlives you requires you to stop obsessing over your own limitations. You are the vessel, not the fuel.

If you want to leave a mark that's still visible in the year 4025, you have to start acting like someone who has the "Greater Things" DNA in their blood. You have to be willing to be a little bit "extra." You have to be willing to do the work that makes people say, "How the hell did they do that?" The answer is always: They didn't. They just let the Big Energy flow through them.

You are an ancestor. The Temple is waiting for your sons and daughters to step up.

Now that you've got the vision for your lasting legacy, there's only one thing left to do. The world is waiting, and you can't hold back.

The next chapter is the final mic drop. It's time to unleash your frequency.

ASAPH MODE

The Vibe Check: Asaph Mode Enabled

Y ou've made it. You know the playbook that Asaph used to dominate in his time—and that you can use to dominate in yours:

1. Activate Authority (Chapter 5): You stop treating God like a distant ATM and start realizing the authority of the throne is in you. You are a royal architect.

2. Tune Your Frequency (Chapter 6): You stop singing other people's songs and find the unique, non-negotiable sound that you were wired to carry.

3. Command Silence (Chapter 10): You learn how to tell the noise, the panic, and the enemy's boast to shut up.

4. Build Your Legacy (Chapter 11): You commit to building a system that outlives you, turning your personal genius into a lasting lineage.

So, what's the big, epic, final lesson? It's not about finding a new technique or reading another dusty scroll. It's about killing the one tiny, whispering lie that still holds you back.

The lie is this: "I'm not ready yet."

Oh, honey. Please.

The "I'm not ready" lie is your ego's last-ditch effort to keep you small and comfortable. It hides in things like, "I need one more certification," or "I need a bigger platform," or "I need to feel less afraid." It's the spiritual equivalent of having a perfectly tuned instrument in your hand and insisting you can't play it until the moon is in the seventh house and you've polished the frets one more time.

Jahaziel didn't wait until the ten nations were gone to act. He didn't wait until he felt safe. He took the only thing he had—his drum, his voice, and his connection—and he used it right in the middle of the fire. He didn't just hope the chaos would subside; he became the cause of the chaos in the enemy camp.

The Final Move: Stop Tuning, Start Playing

The Kingdom doesn't operate on perfection; it operates on presence.

Your divine frequency—that unstoppable sound we talked about—is not a gentle suggestion. It's the original blueprint for reality, and the moment you unleash it, the atmosphere must conform.

Think of it like this: You have the master tuning fork for

your life in your hand. The rest of the world (your bank account, your relationships, your health) is currently playing flat because of fear, worry, and limiting beliefs. You can stand there, looking at your tuning fork and wondering if it's the right color, or you can do what Asaph did:

You strike the frequency, and you trust the physics, or trust the one who created the physics like in Jahaziel's case.

When you speak your truth—when you launch that business, when you heal that relationship, when you declare your health—you are striking your tuning fork. And everything that is vibrating at a lower, flatter frequency must either align or scatter.

This is your final, non-negotiable command: Just hit play.

1. Don't Ask for Approval: Stop asking people (or God, for that matter) if your idea is "good enough" or "safe enough." If it aligns with your authentic sound, it's necessary. Your sound is your permission slip.

2. Don't Wait for the Feeling: Courage isn't the absence of fear; it's the decision to act in spite of the fact that your knees are knocking. Do the declaration, send the email, hit the stage—and then let the courage catch up to you.

3. Start Small, End Massive: Jahaziel started with a drum and a voice. You can start with a single conversation, a single product, a single hour dedicated to your true purpose. It's not the size of the initial spark; it's the consistency of the flame that builds the fire that outlives you.

Your unique, unstoppable sound is the sound of your purpose demanding to be heard. It is the sound that brings order to chaos, silences the enemy, and leaves a lineage of power behind you.

The lie: you need to find yourself to be happy in life.

There's no need to find yourself. Really all you have to do is learn to live.

How to Stop Navel-Gazing and Start Building Heaven)

So, you've got the vision. You've got the "greater things" DNA pulsing through your veins. Now comes the part where most people freak out and go back to scrolling on their phones:

The First Step!

We spend so much time "preparing" and "praying for clarity" that we forget that God responds to **motion, action** (it is impossible to please God without faith, and faith without actions is dead). You don't need a 50-year blueprint; you just need to get on the field and play.

The Marriage Myth (And Why We're Blowing It)

Since we're talking about building things that outlive us, let's talk about the ultimate legacy-incubator: Marriage.

The Christian divorce rate is a hot mess because we've bought into the lie that marriage is a self-service station. We walk down the aisle thinking, "Finally! Someone to meet my needs, laugh at my jokes, and rub my feet." Wrong.

If you go into marriage looking for "The One" to make you happy, you've already lost. Marriage isn't for you. In reality, marriage is a construction site where your job is to build a little piece of Heaven for the person you're marrying. And let me tell you, I know a little something about construction sites. They're dirty, loud, messy, and sometimes things don't go to plan. You have to learn how to work with different trades and on top of that you have to accommodate and compromise your work and your ego so that the other person lays down the foundation that will accommodate your furniture in the future. It's the ultimate "Love Your Neighbor" test, except your neighbor lives in your house and occasionally steals all the covers.

God's Math of Commitment

Forget the 50/50 nonsense. Real marriage is a chaotic, beautiful, "hold-my-breath-and-jump" math equation that looks something like this:

- 80% Sacrifice: (Doing the dishes when it's "not your turn.")

- 20% Running by the seat of your pants: (Because life is a freak show.)

- 50% Grace: (Being in the right place at the right time for your spouse.)

- 100% Unconditional Love: (The glue that holds the madness together.)

Yes, that adds up to way more than 100%. That's the point. It's an overflow.

The Asaph Factor: Lineage and Legacy

Look at Asaph. The guy was a legendary songwriter and leader, but he knew he couldn't do it all in one lifetime. He got married because he knew he needed a lineage (plus it's a Godly thing to do). We don't read too much about his wife but we do know he had one because he had sons. I hope we've had enough instruction to not have to go through the birds and the bees lesson again but the fact is that it's important.

Your marriage is the greenhouse for your dreams. There is potential inside you right now that you will never see come to fruition in your own life. But in your children. In your "mini-mes". That's where your "unrealized" dreams become their reality. You are planting trees whose shade you will never sit under. That's not a tragedy; that's a legacy.

No Spouse? No Problem.

Now, some of you are thinking, "Cool story, Edwin, but I'm single as a Pringle."

Listen: The "Mini-Me" principle isn't restricted to biological offspring. If you aren't married, your mission doesn't change—it just gets wider. You are called to be a Disciple-Maker. Find some kids, find some "newbies" in your field, find someone who is drowning and throw them a rope. Impart your vision into them. Use your gifts to fuel their fire. Whether they share your DNA or just your passion, you are still building a lineage. You are still playing the game.

I have children now but when I was single I made several disciples that now make a living from what I taught them. One is a full time drummer and he tours around the world, another started a sound company in Guanajuato Mexico. Yet another plays at church on Sundays and is starting to get paid gigs. The crazy part is that I didn't show them deep secret techniques and amazing lessons that would make universities come crawling for my curriculum. No. I showed them the door. I spent a few months with them week by week until they had the basics down. And they themselves took their gifts and talents to the next level. They achieved way more than I have achieved just like Jahaziel did compared with Asaph.

Marching Orders

Stop waiting for the "perfect" conditions. The world doesn't need more spectators; it needs people who are willing to get a little messy, make a lot of sacrifices, and build something—anything—that looks like Heaven.

Just play and pray. The rest will take care of itself. If you don't know how to pray, just readd this short prayer...

"God, thank you for giving me the guts to start before I'm ready. Whether I'm building a marriage, a business, or a tribe of mini-mes, help me remember it's not about me—it's about the Heaven I'm leaving behind. I'm stepping onto the field. Let's play."

The Audit of the Century

Let's talk about your "market value" for a second. In our world, things are worth whatever someone is willing to pay for them. If someone pays $500 for a pair of sneakers, those sneakers are "worth" $500.

Now, look at the price tag God himself put on your spouse, your kids, your disciples, and—most importantly—YOU. God didn't just throw some spare change your way. He traded His only Son, Jesus, for you. That is the ultimate "I'm all in" move. If the Creator of the Stars, the universe, the atoms that run you, and the electrons that run those atoms thinks the person sitting across from you at the breakfast table is precious enough to die for, you'd better stop treating them like a "project" or an "inconvenience." They (and you) are a high-stakes investment. Treat them like the royalty they are.

The Audacity of Faithfulness

We live in a "swipe-left' culture. When things get hard, we quit. When the marriage gets boring, we bail. When the kids are acting like tiny monsters, we check out.

But if you want that "outlive-you" legacy, you have to have the audacity to stay. It takes zero effort to walk away. It takes a total, 100% sacrifice to stay faithful to the end.

It takes grit to keep building that "little piece of heaven" when the roof is leaking and the "80% sacrifice" feels more like 99%.

You are valuable because you are the "temple"

Asaph was a genius, but he operated under a restricted model. He had to go to the physical Temple, the appointed place where the presence of God dwelt behind a massive, scary veil. His job was to bring the pure sound to the tent and to the people.

Now here's the cosmic irony: When Jesus hung on the cross, who was still serving in that Temple? The descendants of Asaph. They were still doing the daily duties, the songs, the prayers—the form was perfect, but the fire was missing. The Temple had become a legalistic echo chamber, not a fiery furnace of encounter. The manifest glory (Shekinah) that rested on the original ark? Gone. The prophetic intensity? Drained. The Temple was running on empty ritual.

Then Jesus shouts, "It is finished." The earth shakes, and that massive, thick, dividing veil rips itself from top to bottom. It wasn't just a physical tear; it was the ultimate, cosmic Cancel Button on the old system. The physical structure is obsolete. The geographic restriction is canceled.

Why? Because the Presence stopped waiting for a building to be finished. It chose you.

The Ultimate Upgrade: You Are the Tabernacle

This is the non-negotiable, seismic truth you must embrace: You are the Temple.

You are no longer just an instrument carrying a sound; you are the Sanctuary where the Divine Presence takes up permanent residence. When Jesus died and rose again, the Holy Spirit—the very engine of the Kingdom of God—moved in.

The Old Testament spent centuries preparing a place for God's Presence:

• The Tabernacle was a tent where God's glory rested (Exodus 40:34-35).

• The Ark of the Covenant was the physical chest that housed His manifest presence, and only a select few could even get near it. God's heart was always to dwell with His people.

But look at what the New Testament says about you now:

"Do you not know that your body is a temple of the

Holy Spirit who is in you, whom you have from God, and that you are not your own? For you were bought with a price; therefore glorify God in your body." (1 Corinthians 6:19-20)

The language is uncompromisingly clear. The physical body you walk around in—the one you feed, the one you doubt, the one you power up with coffee—is the absolute center of God's operation on planet Earth.

You aren't carrying a frequency anymore, you are carrying the Presence itself. You don't just ask the Kingdom to come; you are the Kingdom coming.

Holiness is Your Vibe. Praise is Your Rent.

What did God require of the old Temple? Holiness and Praise. He required a pure, dedicated place where He could be glorified without distraction. Guess what? He hasn't lowered the standard; he just made the requirement personal.

If you are the Temple, you have two non-negotiable responsibilities:

1. Keep the Sanctuary Clean (Holiness)

Holiness isn't about rigid rules; it's about separating

yourself from low-frequency living so the Presence of God has room to operate without static. Anything that contaminates your focus, your intention, or your core identity is cluttering the Temple floor.

Your Kingdom DNA (from Chapter 11) is your standard of holiness. You can't be the carrier of the divine sound if you are constantly tuning into the toxic noise of the world. Clean up your space. Your body, mind, and spirit are too sacred for compromise.

2. Sound the Shofar (Praise)

Praise is the only required maintenance for the Temple. When you praise, you are actively acknowledging and magnifying the Presence dwelling inside you. You are striking the tuning fork of heaven and aligning your inner world with your actual reality.

When Asaph and his sons offered praise, walls fell, enemies scattered, and breakthrough was guaranteed. When you offer praise:

• You activate the sound of God that silences the enemy (refer back to Chapter 10).

• You release the Kingdom into your environment, because where the King's presence is, His rule is established.

You don't need a cathedral. You need a mouth and a grateful heart. Your job isn't to get the Presence; it's to release the sound of the Presence already within you.

This is your final, definitive mission statement: You are a moving, speaking, breathing sanctuary. Go walk into every room and every situation knowing that the moment you enter, the Temple has arrived, and the frequencies of heaven must dominate the atmosphere.

Just Hit Play. The sound is already in the Sanctuary.

The Ultimate "Well Done"

Think about the end of the movie. You've played the game. You've sweated, you've sacrificed, you've loved unconditionally even when you wanted to scream into a pillow. You cross that final finish line, and you aren't just met with a participation trophy.

The King of the Universe looks you in the eye and says:

"Well done, good and faithful servant. You stayed in the game. You loved my people. Now, come and check out this kingdom I built specifically for you and your tribe."

That's not just a nice sentiment. That's the reward for

having the guts to live a life that wasn't just about you.

Why You Are Worth It

And hey, while you're busy building this legacy for others, don't forget that you are part of the prize. You are valuable enough to be loved, cherished, and rewarded for eternity. You aren't just a worker bee in God's garden; you're the heir to the whole estate.

So, stop playing small. Stop doubting your worth. Have the audacity to believe that you—yes, **you** (please point at yourself and ask, me?)—were meant to do "greater things" and leave a sound that even time can't stop.

The Big Finale

Asaph wasn't just some guy clashing cymbals in a dusty temple; he was a frequency-shifter. And his vibe was so high that it echoed across centuries, straight into the mouth of Jesus Himself. When the religious elite tried to shut Christ down for being 'too much' and 'too loud', Jesus didn't back down. He reached into Asaph's Greatest Hits and dropped a truth bomb from Psalm 82: 'I said, you are gods.' Think about that. The Messiah didn't quote a rulebook; He quoted a songwriter to remind us that we aren't just meat-suits wandering around—we are divine expressions of God himself. By leaning on Asaph's lyrics, Jesus gave us the ultimate permission slip to own our power. The song Asaph started in the pits of the Old Testament found its mic-drop moment in the New. So, if the Son of God used Asaph's words to prove our divinity, maybe it's time you started believing in your own. The melody is already playing; you just have to be bold enough to sing along.

ABOUT THE AUTHOR

Edwin Santos

Edwin Santos (@freedcmihk) is an independent author, creative architect, and cultural builder whose work sits at the intersection of faith, identity, legacy, and sound. With a background spanning more than two decades in professional audio-visual engineering, music production, and systems design, Santos brings a rare builder's mindset to storytelling—one rooted not just in ideas, but in structure, rhythm, and durability.

He is the author of Asaph Mode, a bold, generational work inspired by the biblical figure Asaph, exploring what it means to become a living instrument—someone whose inner life, discipline, and worship shape outcomes far beyond personal success. Rather than writing for trends, Santos writes for inheritance: his work consistently challenges readers to think in terms of legacy, spiritual architecture, and long-term impact across families and generations.

Beyond the page, Santos is deeply involved in creative production and mentorship. He is a lifelong musician and producer currently developing a multi-song worship album designed to help listeners delight in God through sound, frequency, and presence. His approach to music mirrors his writing—intentional, layered, and rooted in purpose rather than performance.

Santos is also the founder of Freedom In His Kingdom (FreedomIHK), a developing nonprofit initiative focused on equipping youth and young adults with practical creative and technical skills—particularly in music, audio, and production—while providing a safe, purpose-driven environment for growth. His passion lies not in mass appeal, but in transformation: helping people build inner "bulwarks" that allow them to stand firm, create boldly, and lead responsibly.

Known for blending biblical insight with modern language and cultural awareness, Santos' writing style has been described as both grounding and catalytic—bridging ancient truth with contemporary life. His work often draws from architectural metaphors, sound theory, and lived experience, making his books resonate with readers who are tired of surface-level inspiration and hungry for depth.

As an independent author, Edwin Santos is committed to creative ownership, excellence in presentation, and publishing with intention. He believes the future of authorship belongs to builders—those willing to steward both message and medium with integrity.

He lives and creates with his family, continuing to write, produce, and mentor with one driving conviction: what you build within determines what you release into the world.

www.ingramcontent.com/pod-product-compliance
Lightning Source LLC
Chambersburg PA
CBHW022356040426
42450CB00005B/215